They Live On

They Live On: Saying Goodbye to Mom and Dad
Copyright © 2010 by Patricia A. Nugent

Printed in the United States of America

Journal Arts Press • Saratoga Springs, New York

To order additional copies of this title, contact the author at
info@theyliveon.org.

ISBN: 978-0-578-08161-8

They Live On

~

Saying Goodbye to
Mom and Dad

Patricia A. Nugent

Old age is the most unexpected of all the things
that happen to a man.
-Leon Trotsky

How do you get from here to there –
I mean from where I am to the nursing home?
In the snap of the fingers, the blink of an eye.
-Edward Field, *Death Mask*

Contents

Part Three: Four, Please

Part Nine: Just Passing Through

Part Twelve: May God Have Mercy

Part Thirteen: That's Enough 187

Part Fourteen: The Second Time   201

Part Fifteen: The Opening Window   213

Prologue

They Live On was never intended to be a book; it was written as a journal to help me make sense of the 18 months I spent as a caregiver for my parents at the end of their lives.

Neither was it a diary chronicling all events related to their final days. I wrote when the spirit moved me, to help me seek clarity and to help me remember moments that seemed surreal, too beautiful or too terrible to forget. There were sadder times, and there were happier times than recorded here. There were additional visits from relatives and friends that significantly contributed to the experience. And there were too often times when I simply could not put pen to paper, so great the exhaustion and depression.

The transcription of my journal became a series of vignettes portraying the stages of caring for and saying goodbye to a loved one, as seen through the eyes of a daughter and her terminally ill parents. The grieving process is similar for any significant loss, although I believe that the intense grief of an adult losing a parent needs a stronger voice to be appreciated in our culture. Most of us will bear witness to our parents' final days – a task for which I was woefully unprepared.

I struggled with publishing such a personal, intimate story. But as psychologist Carl Rogers observed, the most private of our stories is also the most universal. With encouragement, I came to realize that this is *my* story depicting the universality of the caregiving and grieving cycles – the roller coaster of loss that all of us experience. I wish I had had such a resource when I was in the throes of saying goodbye to help me better understand that the stages of loss are circular, not linear.

Thank you to family and friends, identified by first name, who listened to my story as it unfolded and offered such wise counsel, and to those who read the many drafts and provided commentary. A special thank you to Billy, a friend who became the son my mother never had.

I dedicate this book to those who work in elder care *(Others)* and the wonderful people for whom they care *(Those People)*. They have taught me so much about the journey from life to death.

I apologize in advance for the tears that you may shed as you anticipate or relive your own final goodbyes on these pages. Know that others who have walked the path cry with and for you. And that you will smile again because those we have loved *do* live on.

Patricia Nugent

Part One: The Closing Window

The Closing Window

I thought I was reconciled to my rocky relationship with my father. That I had done all I could to make it right, even though it was far from perfect. Then the call from an emergency room in Florida: "Your father's fallen and broken his hip. But he's OK. At least he didn't hit his head."

Despite my mother's bravado on the phone, we both know what a broken hip means to an old man. Doesn't the end always start with a broken hip? My last visit with him ended in yet another squabble. The few phone conversations since then have been fleeting and meaningless. Has my window closed for further reconciliation with my father? Is this how the relationship will end?

Feeding Tubes

Another call from the hospital: "They want to put feeding tubes in your father. He's not swallowing correctly since the hip surgery, and they're insisting that they must put tubes in. I said no, but they said they must."

My mother is more unglued than I have ever heard her. She is desperate, looking for direction from me, a rare occurrence.

She goes on: "Your father won't tolerate feeding tubes. He'll tear them out. He'd rather die than live like that. I can't let them do this to him."

I agree with her decision and tell her she's right. *But what do I know?*

She is sobbing, scared and distraught: "But they're making me feel terrible for not letting them do this. What if I'm wrong and they're right? What should I do?"

I tell her to trust her instincts and to not let the doctors bully her. I tell her to stand up to them, to hold her ground. *But what do I know?*

"They keep sending different doctors in to try to convince me. But one nurse whispered to me that I was right, that she wouldn't do it either."

"You are right, Mom. Stick to your guns." *But what do I know?*

"I have to go. Here's another doctor." She hangs up, and I fear for her, although it is my dad who is apparently in danger.

I sit and worry thousands of miles away while she battles the medical establishment alone in Florida. But I am confident she is up to the task…although she is exuding a fear and vulnerability I have never before witnessed.

> *My mother prevailed, as usual. Within a few weeks of this episode, my father began to swallow correctly again as a result of speech therapy. Feeding tubes were not necessary after all. Less than one year later, my mother too began aspirating. But I knew, with all certainty, that feeding tubes were out of the question for her. Eighteen months later, I would become the voice opposing the insertion of feeding tubes in my father.*

This Old Man

"I know he's just an old man to you," my mother tells the nurse upon placing my father in a nursing home. "But he was young once like you. He was the captain of his college basketball team and a captain in the Army Air Corps. He was a director of physical education and a coach. And even though he's old now and you don't see him like that, I still do. So I want you to treat him with dignity and respect."

She is choked up as she says this, and I am struck by the tenderness with which she remembers. By the intensity of her commitment, indeed her love. This is a side of my mother I have never seen. Her vulnerability both scares and pleases me. For if she is vulnerable, she is not invincible as I have always believed. Yet if she is not vulnerable, she is less than honest with herself and me.

I typed and framed my mother's words and put it on my father's nightstand. Weeks later, when the doctor told her that it was time to refer my father to Hospice, my mother handed him "This Old Man" to read. She stoically told the doctor, "We'll do what we have to do," and she looked so sad and radiant at the same time.

In Bed, Small

I put down the safety bar and crawl in with my father. He scoots over as best he can to give me room in his narrow bed. I kiss him, and he says, "I love my baby." He strokes my arm as I remember him doing when I was a kid. He then holds up his scrawny arm and says, "You are bigger than I am now."

It is true. I am now bigger than the man who was always bigger than life to me.

That night, I lie alone and small in my parents' bed in Florida while my mother sleeps in the twin bed in the guest room. She hasn't slept in their marital bed since her husband was taken by ambulance from his home two months ago. I sleep in that bed now when I visit, on my father's side, on sheets that still carry my parents' scent. But I don't really sleep.

Goodnight, Dad. Goodnight, Mom. Our family is now scattered. There are pieces of us still around. But "we" are gone. Except in the memories this bed holds.

I leave their bed and crawl into the twin bed with my mother. She lies very still, not acknowledging my presence. She too is so small. And as I hug her, I pray silently to the heavens: *Be gentle with this gentle woman. I love her so.*

The Best Me

How I handle – no, how I participate in – my father's death will define me as a person. I want it to be the best me, one of whom I can be proud when it's over. One who doesn't run from the agony, who doesn't shirk the duty. One who really feels the pain, who lets it hurt and does not seek distraction. One who gives him what he needs and puts all the old wounds aside. I want to be someone my dad is proud of...at last.

Who will they say I am when it all shakes out? Who will I have been? Who am I becoming?

She Stayed

"I want to liberate my mother," I tell him. "I want to convince her that she doesn't have to be by my father's bedside all the time. I want her to have some time without him so she can experience life without being controlled by him."

The therapist listens and points out that it seems to be all about what I want. But what does my mother want? He tells me that there is a 62-year dynamic between my parents that I can't change. He tells me my mother has made choices, and she chose to stay. If my father were to "go," she just might "go" too. He is her raison d'etre.

"What could you offer her instead?" he pointedly asks.

I am silent.

> "How was the party, Mom?"
> "Boring," she responded. "Your father always knew how to liven up a party. It was boring without him."

If I Were in That Chair

My mother always has a kind word to say to the nursing home residents when she visits my father. She calls them by name, tells them they look nice. She advocates for them with the nursing staff.

When I ask why she does it, how she has the energy, she simply responds, "If I were in that chair, I'd want someone to take the time to talk to me."

She tells me she feels a sense of pride that she can come and go from the nursing home as she pleases at the age of 87, can walk on her own unlike most of the residents. It makes her feel somewhat guilty to be prideful, but she is grateful that she is still independent. Although she frequently falls asleep in a chair while visiting her husband.

> When she ended up "in that chair," she showed no interest in engaging with her fellow residents. Yet she remarked to me on how friendly I was to them. I was simply doing what she modeled.

This is Tough

> *"What are you thinking, Dad?"*
> *"That I'm all finished."*
> *"Why do you think that?"*
> *"Because I can't do anything."*

"Can't I go with you?" my father asks as I am saying goodbye once again to head to the airport. He is disappointed when he hears the answer and perturbed that he can't be a gracious host and see me off. He assumes my mother is taking me to the airport while he is left behind, unaware that she no longer feels confident enough to do so. Instead, I will be taking a shuttle.

Today, his agitation turns to tears.

"This is tough," he says. "This is tough. But go ahead. I love you."

"I love you too, Dad," I respond. And then I leave him to fly home, thousands of miles away.

Watching Her Go

The schism in our relationship is deeper than ever. After spending three days together with our parents in Florida, it's time to say goodbye to my sister – perhaps for a long time.

Limited time and the reason for our joint visit should have resulted in a bonding experience. But such is not to be; we are so different. She disparagingly says I am like Mom, and she is like Dad. We see the world, our parents, and ourselves very different-ly. Even when we try to comfort each other in our parallel grief, it doesn't work as we seem to say all the wrong things to each other. We each call friends for support instead of turning to each other.

There is no room for me when she is around. She seems to recoil at my having any status – much less equal status – in the family. I try to become invisible so as not to be an irritant or a target. And then sometimes, I play up the role of Goody Two Shoes just to annoy her.

We ride in silence to the airport. As soon as we get through the security check, we head in different directions without a word of farewell. I can see her at her gate, and I am resigned to not saying goodbye. I am sad but somehow relieved that the tension – the pretense – is over.

But as I am standing at my gate, she suddenly appears at my side. In silence, we both sit down. She tells me that we have a lot to face together over the next few years, and we need to work out our relationship. I nod.

Her flight is called and this time, I follow her to her gate, not wanting this moment of reconciliation to end. She hugs me and tells me she loves me. I reciprocate and walk away. I watch her though; I see her look around for me, wave and smile.

My tears come as I watch her board. I realize how alone we each feel in dealing with our parents' ordeal. When I board my plane, I tell two perfect strangers my parents' story, and they offer words of comfort. It seems that all it takes is compassion without competition to appreciate the universality of the human condition. Why can't I have that with my own sister?

The Nightly Call

I call my mother every night now to ask how her day went. She always sounds exhausted yet declares that she is fine. Except not so tonight.

She stumbles and hesitates with her answer: "Well, I didn't do so well today. I had numbness on my left side, so I went to the emergency room. They told me I had a little stroke…or a brain tumor. I told them I don't have a brain tumor, so they told me to eat two bananas a day for potassium and to take aspirin, and they sent me home. I'll be OK, dolly. Now don't worry!"

She tries to sound casual, but her voice belies confidence. We continue to talk for a while, convincing each other that she will be fine. *Of course she doesn't have a brain tumor!*

But her bravado is no longer working for either of us.

Years later, I still wonder why the hospital would have sent an 87-year-old with those symptoms home from the emergency room. Or did she just get up and leave?

Dear Mom

Dear Mom,

This letter is to let you know that we will get through this difficult time and that I am available to help you any time you need assistance. Promise me that you will call upon me, and don't worry about being a burden. I would do anything in the world for you.

You have always been there for me, and I have always known I could depend on your strength. Your influence has given me a strong spirit and a strong will. But sometimes we can be too strong – we can make it look easy so that others don't know we need help. But everyone needs support, and I implore you to accept what others want to provide you at this time. You don't have to do this alone, nor should you. Don't let your pride and independence get in the way.

You have done all you can for Dad. It is so sad that he is so helpless and dependent now. But if we are honest, we'll admit that he's been that way for a long while. You've "covered" for him by doing much to keep him active, at great expense to yourself. While the devotion you show is admirable, you must take care of yourself now.

We will solve whatever problems are presented to us. Our best options will become obvious as time unfolds – there are still so many variables that it's hard to sort them all out right now. But we will. I know you get discouraged, and that's understandable. You've been through a lot, and you are under so much stress. But try not to let it get you down. Imagine good things instead of worrying about bad. Envision life getting better for you.

You always advised me to not project out too far but to take each experience as it comes. I return that advice to you. Take it one day at a time – each day will bring different experiences, both good and bad. So when one day is bad, you know a good day is around the corner. And, sadly, the reverse is also true. Remember your mantra: Life is hard, by the yard. By the inch, it's a cinch.

Take heart, Mom. But cry when you need to…you'll feel better afterward. Know that I cry with you and hold you close to my heart. I love and respect you – you are my best friend. I will be there whenever you need me.

                    Love,
                    Patty

Cry into the Darkness

Cry into the darkness.
Feel your pain as you gaze into the night sky.
Beg the moon and the stars for mercy.

Feel small and inconsequential.

Face your dark night, recognizing that this is where you are
to be right now.

Feel the full impact of hope and disappointment.

And wonder if they are mutually exclusive.

Cry, mourn.

Remember the stages of loss.

Remember the stages of life.

Que Sera, Sera

A dark night.

A worried dawn.

Restlessness, anxiety, depression.

Life's permutations running through my head.

Then a realization that life will unfold as it will unfold.

Things will be what they will be.

Lying in bed and worrying does not help the situation.

It only jeopardizes my own physical and mental health.

For, as Doris Day sang, *tomorrow's not ours to see...*

Part Two: Your Mama is Gone

Your Mama is Gone

"Your life goes through stages," my mother had told me two years prior. "You just have to accept it when you leave one stage behind." Easier said than done.

"Don't remember me like this," she instructs me. "Remember me as I was 15 years ago. Not like this. Your mama is gone."

She cries, collapsing in my arms: "Everything went wrong in my life all of a sudden. It's all so overwhelming. I really needed someone, and you came. Thank you."

In short order, she collects herself as she always does and says, "It'll all work out. I'm OK." But she's not. And I'm not.

My mama *is* gone. She is fading away, slipping away from me. And I am powerless, as is she. It runs contrary to all we have been to, and know of, each other. We are learning the ultimate lesson of our lifetimes – we are not really in control. Life unfolds, and we participate to varying degrees.

Tomorrow, I will again fly back to New York State, leaving my mother alone again to care for herself and her infirm husband.

She's Come Undone

"I got so old so quickly," my mother laments. It's an odd comment that rings true. Up until my dad's accident, my mom was a very young 87-year-old, physically and mentally. She looked great and was sharp as a tack. But the resulting stress and depression from a radical change in lifestyle have aged her so rapidly, as if her DNA has come undone.

"It seems you can only outrun old age for so long," I respond. "But you gave it one hell of a run, Mom."

> *In retrospect, I should have realized that she herself might be ill. There were so many clues, but I just couldn't face it.*

Confession

"I feel so guilty," she sobs. "Your father has so much life left in him, and he's in a nursing home. But I just can't take care of him."

While it's true that my mother can no longer care for my father at home, it is soon revealed that her guilt goes deeper.

"I couldn't take his nasty comments anymore," she confesses. "He was terrible to me all morning the day he fell, and I was so desperate that I called upon my parents to help me cope. That afternoon, your father and I went for a walk, and he fell and broke his hip."

She continues: "I thought I wanted to be free of him. But now, I'm still not free, and he's not free. It's a terrible mess."

I don't know what to say. I tell her this isn't her fault, that it was an accident. Yet I am startled by her confession.

Was that you? I wonder silently to my deceased grandparents.

Did you do that for your daughter? If so, please, I implore you, continue to watch over her. But leave her here with me for a while longer...and now please help my dad.

Only Make-Believe

The shuttle drops me off again at the Tampa Airport. I sit at my gate and cry – sob actually. I cry because my father still asks (from his nursing home wheelchair) why I won't let him drive me to the airport. I cry because my mother doesn't ask anymore because she knows she can't. I cry because I'm never sure if I'm going to see either one of them again. I cry because of things said and unsaid. I cry because I can never do enough, be enough, to make it all turn out OK. I cry because I feel so alone and scared – and so are my parents. I cry because it seems there is nowhere to turn.

Strangers try not to stare. I mentally run down the list of people to call for comfort. I decide either I have imposed too much already or I just don't want to get into it. I then realize that only my mother can make me feel better. Only my mother's strong confident voice can soothe me. So I call her.

"I'm OK," she reassures me. "Nothing's going to happen to me." And I pretend she can really promise me that – and make it come true. So I stop crying until I write this and realize it's only make-believe. But she knew exactly what I needed to hear. As always.

Years later, she can still make me feel better. I reach for my cell phone and replay the only recording I have of her voice. It is comforting even now, in a magical and bizarre way.

Her Heart Gave Out

*A study conducted at Johns Hopkins has proven that
a broken heart can kill you. The phenomenon is called
stress cardiomyopathy – but I have enough anecdotal
evidence to convince me without this formal research.*

"Doris died," my mother informs me on the phone. "She just got
real sick. We thought it was a cold, but then her heart gave out."

Despite her affinity for this nursing home resident, my mother sounds matter-of-fact in her delivery, perhaps reflecting her
heightened awareness of her peers' (and her own) mortality. But
I am devastated by the news. Doris was in great shape before Ed
took ill. But apparently "her heart gave out" soon after. Like Ro-
meo and Juliet.

Less than three weeks before, when we took Doris to see Ed in
the hospital, I could see her heart begin to break. She wanted to
kiss him but was told he may be contagious. So she stood with her
walker next to his bed and told him of her love.

"Don't cry," she told him. "We'll be together again soon." But
he did cry, and so did she.

Ed eventually recovered and came back to their joint room in
my father's nursing home. They'd sit together on the couch holding hands. But then Doris's heart just "gave out."

"Aren't you glad now that you did that good deed for Doris?"
my mother asks after telling me of her death.

Truth is, I had resisted taking Doris to see Ed in the hospital,
feeling that we had enough problems of our own. I didn't understand why my mother would extend herself even more, and
I begrudged any additional expenditure of time or energy, given
our own dire straits.

"I'm glad you *made* me do it, Mom," I respond. "I never would have offered on my own. Thank you."

Maybe I'm Crazy

"Maybe I'm crazy," she says. "But I really like being with your father."

She tells me this as we return from the Mothers' Day tea at his nursing home. But she doesn't have to tell me; it was quite obvious as I observed their interaction. She reached for his hand; he kissed hers.

"He always was a beau brummel," she says appreciatively. Although she paid a price for that, she apparently enjoyed it as well.

I am witnessing the end of their love story. And perhaps for the first time, I am beginning to understand their relationship.

Keep Going

My mother has decided to stay in Florida year-round to be near my father. While I'm packing up their apartment in New York State, my cell phone rings, lighting up with the ID "Mom."

"Hi Mom," I cheerfully answer, pleased that she has called to help me make decisions regarding her belongings.

"Patty, it's Shelby," the voice on the other end says.

Shelby? Why would my mother's friend be using her cell phone?

"What's wrong?" I demand to know without social protocol.

"Well, we stopped over to visit your mother and found her lying on the bathroom floor. We called 911."

I instantly know that this changes everything. I call my sister who says she will catch the next flight out from Wisconsin to Florida. I then collapse, unable to function, unable to continue the mundane and pointless process of packing up my parents' possessions. My cousin Shannon tells me to keep going: "You have a job to do, and you don't know how the story ends yet. Keep going, keep going."

I Can't Hug Him

"It's just a little stroke. It's not a brain tumor," she insists. "And even if it is, it won't grow very fast at my age."

The MRI is inconclusive, but the neurosurgeon believes it is indeed a brain tumor. He tells my mother she should have a biopsy immediately. She refuses.

"I just don't trust him," she tells me. "Dr. Bernie Siegel says you shouldn't work with a doctor you don't feel you can hug. Well, I can't hug him, and I don't want him doing the biopsy."

She is so convincing, so strong, that I acquiesce. We agree that we will have it done back in New York State after she regains some strength.

The doctor is dismayed. "Just don't wait too long," he warns me. "In two weeks, your mother is going to be a very sick woman."

Unfortunately, she heard him.

> *Although at this time my mother could still walk, two weeks later I had to carry her through the airport. Was the doctor that accurate or did it become a self-fulfilling prophesy?*

We Can't Stay Here

She is simply languishing in this Florida hospital. Each time I see her, I think I see evidence of creeping paralysis; today the left side of her mouth seems to be drooping. And she is despondent.

I visit by day and sleep alone in my parents' bed at night – desperate lonely nights, howling like an animal with sobs so deep I can barely catch my breath. If she is not dying, then I surely must be.

Unable to sleep, I call my sister at 3am. We discuss options and decide that I should take her back to New York State immediately, "to a good hospital" so we can get to the bottom of this and make her well.

As soon as offices open, I call several neurosurgeons in Albany and am fortunate to get an appointment for the very next day.

My mother says she wants to go back to New York but insists she can't leave Florida yet. She must first clean out her home and turn in her leased car. Most importantly, she cannot leave her husband alone in Florida.

I tell her the plane reservations and doctor appointments have been made, and we're leaving early tomorrow morning.

This is the first time she has not been in control. And it may be the first time that I don't want to be.

Willing

> "I heard about someone whose brain tumor shrunk
> following a plane ride. Maybe that will happen to me,"
> she said during our flight, signifying that she knew the
> truth, despite her words of denial.

On the plane, after "kidnapping" my mother out of the hospital against doctor's orders, I realize that I love her enough to be willing to trade places with her.

That realization is shocking to me. I have never before realized a willingness to die for someone. Yet I know I would die for my mother.

She has been whisked away so quickly from all that she knows, in all likelihood never to return to her Florida home. There was no time to say goodbye to her husband. And knowing what she will be facing medically, physically and emotionally, I am willing to die in an airplane crash with her should it happen on our way to yet another hospital. I almost wish for it.

> *"Didn't I tell you everything would be OK if we could just get back to New York? I still believe that," she told me months later. She searched my eyes for signs of hope. I wonder if she found any there.*

Clothes are Stupid

I look in my closet and think how insignificant clothes are right now. What does it matter what I wear to see my failing mother in the hospital? What does it matter how I look to attend her biopsy?

My mother's clothes have all been shipped to my home and hang in a closet, naively awaiting her arrival. Will she ever again be out of bed, much less wear clothes?

Clothes are stupid.

The Room

"I have the biopsy results. I'll meet you in the conference room to discuss them."

I hang up the phone in the nurses' station, numb but fully aware of the implication. A face-to-face meeting with a very busy neurosurgeon signals a significantly negative outcome.

I can see the conference room from where I am standing but don't know if my legs can carry me there. My insides are writhing.

By somehow putting one foot ahead of the other, I arrive first and peer into the room. *So this is where I'm going to hear that my mother's tumor is malignant. This is where our lives turn upside down, in this little unpretentious room. To think that such a place could be the setting for such disturbing news.*

The doctor arrives and takes a seat; I do not. I pace. I do not want him to say the words out loud.

Not only is it malignant, but it is also aggressive. Radiation will help, he tells me.

I barely hear him.

Sometime later, I realize I am alone in the room.

The Pledge

My sister and I meet for dinner, and I tell her of the biopsy results. We immediately outline how we will save her: *What about that cab driver who said he had healing powers? Nutrition therapy? Radiation? We'll try it all. It will work. It has to! She's our mom!*

We agree that our mother is not to be told that the tumor is malignant, for fear she will just give up. After all, she wouldn't let the doctor tell my father he had prostate cancer years before, and he beat that! So that's the way it will be.

We hold hands over the table in the middle of the restaurant and make a solemn pledge that we will save her. Together, we can do it!

The Telling

We sit as in a classroom, my mother alone in the front row, facing the radiologist. My aunt, sister and I sit behind her. He gently explains that she has a brain tumor but, at our request, avoids the words "malignant" or "cancer." He tells her it is inoperable, but radiation will help shrink it.   Questions are asked regarding other treatment options, of which there are none. We do not ask about time remaining.

I can't see her face, only the back of her head, held high as always. The only question I specifically remember her asking is "Will I lose my hair?" which is answered affirmatively. She says that's OK, she likes hats anyway.

He leaves, and we discuss her options, including going to a brain tumor center. She tells us she will do the radiation here because it will help.

From there, we go directly to the hospital cafeteria, where most of our food is left on the trays when we leave.

"At least I'm not dying," she says to me later. "All I've got is this brain tumor. I'm OK other than that."

Her spirit is indomitable.

Something Bigger

By following a path less traveled (made possible by a vandalized fence), I find myself overlooking a waterfall. The torrential currents rushing by seem to come from out of nowhere. My stomach turns over when I peer down, awed by the power and the danger that lie below.

Dryphuss, my golden retriever, is neither cowed nor afraid of his precarious position. Although it is hard for this four-legged creature to navigate the narrow passages, he accepts the currents as part of his natural world, not something to be feared. He puts his face to the wind and stands as close to the edge as he can. I hold onto him, of course, afraid for his oblivion. But I soon realize that I am afraid for myself, not for him. I am out of my element, vulnerable to my surroundings. Power and control are not mine.

I pray to the infinite universe, to the gods of power and might, to the elements, to all who came before me on these sacred grounds. I pray for my mother, for healing, for strength. And I allow myself to accept that I need help, that I believe in something bigger than I.

Sunset

> A nurse told me that nursing home residents "sunset" at dusk, becoming more restless and more desperate. I did too.

Don't go, I beg the setting sun. *Stay with me. Warm my dog and bring me sunshine.* Because sunshine represents hope and light. It's hard to feel desperate when the sun is shining down upon you.

The sun has been my companion all day. But now it sinks lower in the sky even as I plead with it not to leave me. Because darkness will bring demons – inner demons that remind me that all is not well in my world. The sun holds them at bay but can only protect me for so long.

I begin to feel the chill of the sun's departure; Dryphuss sleeps through it. Maybe if you don't see something leave, you don't feel the loss quite as much.

Don't draw the shades tonight. I want sunlight to fill the bedroom in the morning, to dispel my despair. I want sunlight to pierce my closed eyelids, reminding me that a new day has dawned and that it's safe to get out of bed.

Don't let me wake up in a dark room. My heart is dark enough already. I need the sunlight to fool me into beginning anew tomorrow.

Who Hasn't Prayed?

Who hasn't prayed for a loved one to get better?
Who hasn't sent a desperate plea to the heavens to be spared
    loss and suffering?
Who among us hasn't asked for divine intervention?
Who doesn't hope to escape unscathed?

Is it futile to think your plea might be special or that you can
    bargain for more time?
It works for some.
And what is left if you surrender such delusions?
Only the stark reality of the inevitability of death.

Prayer feels like my only hope.

I No Longer Believe

> *"You did have a charmed life," Patti Jo told me. "It's just
> that it doesn't last forever. It goes in cycles. Bad things
> happening doesn't mean you didn't have a charmed life
> and might yet again."*

I no longer believe that bad things won't happen to me.
That my life is charmed, that "that stuff" only happens to other
    people.
I no longer believe that I am somehow protected from tragedy.
I have lost my feeling of being special.
I have lost my innocence.
I have joined the rest of humanity.

Part Three: Four, Please

Four, Please

There is no "good" floor to have as your destination in this hospital known for its state-of-the-art treatments. Most visitors and patients look anxious here. As the elevator door opens to let passengers exit, the floor signs announce why: cardiology, intensive care, neurosurgery, rehabilitation.

Whenever I request "Four, please," I know it is the worst floor on which to be visiting my mother: *Oncology*. I can almost feel the sympathy oozing forth from my fellow passengers as I get off.

Even though she's been here for more than a month, she doesn't know Oncology is her floor because she doesn't know the brain tumor is malignant. We chose not to tell her because she must have a reason to fight – to take the IV's and medications. To show up for the seismic pounding of radiation even though she says it is "squeezing all my brains out." To wake up and face her growing paralysis as they move her around like a rag doll.

We are dealing with what the doctor termed "a lousy diagnosis and a lousy prognosis." But we still shield her – shield ourselves – from that truth at this time.

Touch Down

I wait at the jetway, having been given a special pass to meet him. He is the last one off the plane, wearing a bright red sweater and a straw hat. The nurse we paid to accompany him pushes his wheelchair down the ramp. He waves to me weakly, looking confused and exhausted from the flight from Tampa to Albany.

We collect the luggage and get him into the car. I am surprised when he asks if we can go see my mother right away, assuming he would not fully understand what is going on. As we head off to his new nursing home, I tell him that we will see her tomorrow. He is too tired to protest.

After being abandoned in Florida for over a month while we waited for a room to open up, my father will soon see his wife again. However, he will also sadly learn that the circumstances are far from ideal.

I get him settled into his new residence and leave him – scared and alone yet again. I then run off to the hospital to check on his wife, who is deeply concerned about his welfare.

Reunited

I don't want him to see her lying in a hospital bed. So I leave him alone in the lobby of the hospital and race up to the fourth floor to get her. The aides know she is being reunited with her husband today so they have dressed her up for the occasion. She doesn't know what awaits, only that I am taking her somewhere.

My father has sat nervously humming, a trademark of his. As we approach the lobby, she says, "If I didn't know better, I'd swear I hear your father." We round the corner, and she immediately spots him. When their eyes meet, they both start sobbing. As I self-consciously look around the crowded lobby, I see onlookers also starting to dab their eyes. Mom and Dad try to hug, but their wheelchairs won't permit it.

"You look real good, Nicky," she tells him, stroking his arm.

"Can't you walk?" he asks her bluntly. For although he is in a wheelchair, he doesn't expect her to be.

"Not yet," she responds. "But they're going to fix me up, aren't they, Patty?"

Exhibit A

The king and queen tried to protect their daughter from the curse of the uninvited 13th fairy. They destroyed every spinning wheel in the kingdom. But Briar Rose found the single spinning wheel they had missed, pricked her finger, and fell into a deep sleep.

Something tells me to visit my mother early this morning. Yet it seems uneventful enough as I sit on her bed enjoying a pleasant conversation. I leave to get her some tea and when I return minutes later, she is hysterical. A doctor she had never before met had just walked in with a group of medical students and announced to them that this patient has a brain tumor and has less than six months to live.

I become enraged, a wild animal protecting her cub. I run after the entourage doing rounds and find them down the hall. In front of his students, I scream at the doctor, "Did you really mean to shatter any hope my mother has of surviving? Who do you think you are to decide how long someone can and will live? Bernie Siegel says no doctor can predict that."

He takes me aside while I continue my tirade, but I make sure I am loud enough for his students to hear. He defends his actions but finally agrees to return to her bedside and apologize, noting that he isn't her doctor and isn't totally familiar with her case. Exactly my point.

My mother weeps the rest of the day, despite everyone's best efforts to restore her hope.

> *The doctor's six month prognosis became a reality. Was this another self-fulfilling prophecy?*

Dear Medical Staff

> *Family requests that patient's diagnosis and/or prognosis not be discussed with or in front of patient in the absence of a family member. Thank you.*

> *Dear Medical Staff:*
> *Because of the very disturbing experience my mother and I had on Monday, we received permission for this sign to be posted over her bed. We do this so that this will never happen to her again or to any other vulnerable patient. I request a follow up conversation with the doctor to better clarify our position but until such time, this sign will protect my mother when her loved ones cannot.*
> *There are many lessons for students to learn in a teaching hospital – and humanism and compassion are two very important life-saving treatments. Those were absent in the exchange between the doctor and my mother; as a result, a woman's determination to keep going has turned into despair. We are now trying to restore hope and a reason for her to keep going. So much disappointment and heartbreak could have been avoided by better knowing the patient and incorporating the family into the healing circle.*

Please hang this sign over her bed as a reminder of
the family's request. Thank you for what you do on a
daily basis to make life a little brighter for Amelia. We
must all continue to try to strengthen her against the
odds.

$$\text{Sincerely,}$$
$$\text{Patricia Nugent}$$

We Have Tonight

We eat Wendy's hamburgers and carrot cake. We lie in bed together and watch the Democratic candidates' debate. We comment and laugh, always in sync with each other. I perform reiki on her. We have tonight…together.

There is no other place I would rather be tonight than with my mother…if only it weren't in the hospital.

In the morning, she awoke with a fever and was
diagnosed with pneumonia. We had last night.

What's Best?

"I stayed up all night wondering how I was going to tell you that I'm dying," my mother says in greeting me this morning. "The doctor said my pneumonia is getting worse."

Our request to be present when her condition is discussed has obviously been violated, so I head off in frantic search of the doctor. He explains that my mother must have misinterpreted his morning status report because he had told her that her lungs were, in fact, clearing. *(Gee, maybe this is a good example of why we hung that sign over her bed!!)*

I report the good news back to my mother. Yet I know it's time to talk about dying. I tell her that losing her will be very hard for me, but when it's time, I will help her pass over.

"I only want what's best for you, Mom," I tell her. "I will help you when the time comes."

"Well, I really don't think dying would be best for me right now!" she retorts. We laugh a hard-earned laugh.

It's Up to Me

I hover.
I worry.
I anxiously stand guard.
It's up to me to save her.
I know what to do,
I have been at her side for three months.
I know what works.

I try to control it all…but I can't. Not without totally surrendering my own life – and not even then. "You're doing so much for me, dolly," she says. "I hate to be such a problem for you."

"It's my privilege to help you," I say. But more wearily than I have said those words in the past. If only I could make it all better.

After all, it's up to me, isn't it?

We Stand in the Hallways

We stand in the hallways.
And wait.
We watch the nurses and aides pass by.
We try to get their attention.
Yet try not to be too bold or demanding.
Because we are dependent on their care for our loved ones.

Our loved ones lie in bed.

And wait.

They watch people and monitors come and go.

They try to decipher what is being done to their bodies.

Yet try not to seem too scared or needy.

Because they are dependent on whoever enters their room.

So we stand in the hallways.

And wait.

Health care resources are scarce.

And we have a different view of acceptable care and timing.

We take the role of advocate seriously.

Because we know what can happen if we don't.

Get Her Out of Here!

She stops me in the hallway and pulls me into a conference room. "Get her out of here!" she says. "Hospitals are dirty places. You run a high risk of your mother catching more infections and getting sicker if she stays. Her immune system is compromised from the radiation. If there's any way you can do it, get your mother out of here. Take her home and then take her to radiation every day."

My head is spinning: *How can you get sicker in a hospital? That doesn't make any sense.* I call a friend who is an infection control specialist, and she confirms that despite their best efforts, hospitals are *indeed* dirty places, and I should seriously consider the doctor's advice.

I tell my mother that we may take her home and transport her to radiation every day. She is anxious and says that would be too hard on her and on us. She says she'd rather "stay put."

*After researching our options, her paralysis prevented us
from taking her home and commuting, as we would not
have been able to get her in and out of a vehicle. I still
wish we had.*

Claims Denied

In my mail is a notice from my parents' health insurance carrier denying payment for my mother's brain biopsy and radiation treatments. The reason given is because my parents have been living "out of network" for over six months.

They have been living out of the network for over six months because they got sick and couldn't return home! They had to live near me so that they would have a caregiver. Isn't that when you need health insurance the most?

I sit here with thousands and thousands of dollars worth of unpaid medical bills. On top of everything else.

HOW CAN YOU DO THIS? I want to scream at the insurance company. *THIS ISN'T THEIR FAULT! THEY DIDN'T INTEND TO GET SICK! THEY WOULD LOVE NOTHING MORE THAN TO BE "IN NETWORK" AGAIN.* But instead, I have to make nice, hoping they will take pity on us.

*My brother-in-law, an attorney, was able to file an
appeal to get the claims paid. I then had to find another
health insurance carrier who would take a brain tumor
patient. A challenging task, to say the least.*

Screaming

My father and I are in his room, screaming at each other. Screaming. He wants to get out of there, to go "home." He asks why his wife hasn't come to see him when he's come all the way back from Florida. He asks if there is "someone else."

I am at my wits' end, torn between two parents in two different facilities based on their medical needs and available rooms. I am only one person, running as fast as I can between the two.

I scream at him: "MOM HAS A BRAIN TUMOR, DAD. A BRAIN TUMOR. SHE'S DYING, OK? CAN'T YOU THINK ABOUT SOMEONE ELSE FOR A CHANGE?"

I instantly regret telling him that way; it just slips out. But it doesn't seem to impact him. The head nurse comes in to calm us down. The door to his room is open, and apparently everyone could hear us. She suggests I leave, and she'll take care of him.

I quickly gather up my stuff and run down the hall, crying. I can hear him yelling after me, "Get me out of here!! Patty? Get me out of here."

> *He later disclosed to me that a resident had "flashed" him at lunch, and "that just wasn't right." An investigation was done during which he pointed out a very dignified looking man to the staff, but there was no reason to believe it really happened. Yet...why would he make that up?*

I've Come Undone

> *"Mother and daughter," the passerby declared, looking at my mother and me. "How did you know?" I asked her. "Why, you're carbon copies!" she replied. "Thank you," I responded. And I meant it, after so many years of resisting any resemblance.*

I seem to be mirroring my mother's plight. My throat, my arm, my leg, my memory – all seem to be suffering from her symptoms. I literally feel her pain so much. She is part of me, my second skin. I am one with her. Because of this, I now realize that perhaps there has been no room for my sister or father, a regrettable situation.

I feel so desperate. My energy level has been depleted, my spirit dampened. I am not tending to my own health needs – I only care about hers. Because I have never loved anyone so much. I am her child.

I suddenly feel like a middle-aged woman who is taking care of her parents, which is exactly who I have become ("I got so old so quickly"). Yet I intend to be able to say, "I have no regrets" when my mother's last breath is drawn.

Whose Ethics?

They call me at work to summon me to an ethics hearing at the hospital this afternoon, charged with interfering with a patient's right to know the truth about her medical condition. I arrive and tell my mother that the doctors are mad at me regarding the incident the other day when the medical students were all in her room. I ask her if she agrees that she wants a family member present when the doctors explain something about her condition.

"Yes," she says emphatically. "I want someone else to hear it too in case I don't fully understand." After all, she does have a brain tumor.

I tell her I'll be back after the meeting. That's when she decides she is going too, to defend her daughter.

I walk on ahead, with my mother trailing as the nurse wheels her down the hall. But when I arrive at the meeting room, they are no longer behind me. My mother arrives a few minutes later with a red hat on, which she had asked the nurse to return to her room to get. She tells me it is "my power hat to take on the doctors."

At the meeting, they address all their questions to her, although she had not been invited to attend. She is strong and articulate, defending my right to protect her as I see fit. I don't know if she fully understands what is happening, but the doctors certainly do.

The charge is dropped.

Transcendence

I believe I must transcend my hurt and anger toward my sister if my mother is to transcend her illness.

I want my sister to acknowledge all that I am doing for my parents while she resides out of state – to simply tell me I'm doing a good job. I know I shouldn't need external recognition – it should be enough for me to know that I am doing the best I can.

But I need reinforcement and support. I am so alone.

Alas, my sister and I were not able to transcend our differences in our parents' lifetimes.

Done

The radiation treatments are done. She's told she was "a real trooper" as she always had a smile on her face through the agonizing process. She gets a certificate, hugs, and lots of praise.

What she didn't get was any relief from the paralysis on her left side. There has been no noticeable improvement in her condition. She is bald and traumatized but otherwise unchanged from treatment. Yet they tell us there's still the possibility that the residual radiation in her body will "kick in."

Tomorrow she leaves for a rehab nursing home, so I throw her a going away party after ten weeks in the hospital. My husband Peter toasts her: "The hard part is over, Amelia. Things will get easier from now on."

I can't help but notice the doctors' discomfort when those words are spoken. But I find a way to dismiss it in order to face the next leg of the journey. Naïve, foolish or hopeful, I'm not sure. I just hope we're not wrong.

Time

Thirty-four radiation treatments. Six weeks. Would they ever be done? Counting the days until August 19. The slowest summer, the longest summer, the worst summer. Time stood still, days dragged on. July and August seemed like an eternity, those precious summer months spent anxiously waiting for a reprieve from the disease.

Yet now, with treatments over, the days fly by as we wait out the period during which we might still see some improvement from all that radiation floating around in her body. And every day, there is nothing. Nothing. But ironically, time now races to the deadline where hope must be forsaken. And I wonder why we put her through all that.

> She remained so incredibly sharp even after 34
> radiation treatments to the brain. But she did become
> much sadder...

Part Four: The Ministry of Presence

The Ministry of Presence

"You'll have something so precious when this is all over," the chaplain tells me. "You'll have had the opportunity to be with your mother at the end of her life. It's called the ministry of presence."

I DON'T WANT THIS SO-CALLED OPPORTUNITY, I scream inside. *I DON'T WANT IT! IT'S AWFUL – I WOULD GLADLY GIVE IT AWAY!*

Or would I? Would I forfeit snuggling with my mother in her bed or wiping her tears that break my heart and hers? Would I walk away from the opportunity to comfort my mother? Am I not truly grateful to see her every day, even though we are both in a diminished state?

Names on Clothes

I never thought my mother would end up in a nursing home. As she aged, she told me more than once, "Don't let me ruin your life. Put me in a home if I get bad."
I swore I never would because I never believed this vibrant woman would "get bad." Yet, here we are.

I take the black marker to my mother's stylish clothes. It's a ritual that happens when people live communally for any length of time – like in summer camp, boarding schools, and…nursing homes.

I had watched my mother label my father's clothes with our name just a few months before and was reminded of the same happening with my grandmother and aunt before that.

And now it is my mother's clothes I label for her stay in the nursing home. The clothes that once hung in her closet no longer have their own home. Nor will they get special washing treatment. So I hold back some of "the good clothes" once again, as she always did, and prepare the others for communal living.

NUGENT, I write in big bold letters.

And day by day, the clothes become more stained and gray. The yellow nightgown I gave her, the one she saved "for good," is no longer recognizable. And soon, I fear, she won't be either as this disease continues to take its toll.

A High Rate of Return

I call the president of my local independent bank and tell him that my mother has become incapable of handling her business affairs, and I don't know what to do. Bill listens to my story and suggests he meet with her directly to determine her wishes.

Over lunch at the nursing home, my mother warns Bill that "those corporate banks" always buy out whatever small bank she puts her money in. Bill assures her that he will work hard to prevent that from happening this time. She grins.

A legend is born when my aunt calls the nursing home and is told that her sister is not available, as she is down the hall having lunch with the bank president! What a high rate of emotional return Bill has given my mother, at a time when her pride has been all but stripped. I am so grateful and will remember the value of supporting small independently-owned businesses.

Phone as Enemy

How I used to love getting phone calls, especially on my cell phone! After all, I gave that number out discriminately so only my closest friends had access. And when it would ring, I would be delighted.

No more. The phone now signals distress, as doctors, nurses, and aides call to give or get information. It has become an anchor, a burden – a necessary evil. I am filled with dread every time it rings, hold my breath through voice mails. The phone now scares me – bad things can happen any time of day.

Will the phone be the vehicle by which I hear of the death of a parent? Will I one day soon say "hello" only to be greeted with the most devastating of news? If only I could stop the phone from ringing before that time comes. Perhaps then, I'd never know such grief.

Raccoon Eyes

I've stopped wearing mascara. My tears blend with the make-up to create "raccoon eyes" so I've stopped applying it.

But I still think about it every morning. I try to figure out if I might be able to get through the day without crying. I scroll through the possibilities of what might happen…and usually decide that I shouldn't apply it. Because the potential for tears is there each and every day now. From my own exhaustion to disturbing medical news, tears are easily triggered.

There is no way to predict whether tears will flow. So for now, the mascara should not.

> *I was not able to wear mascara again until after*
> *her funeral.*

The Hardest Thing

> *"I feel sorry for you," my mother said to Peter and me*
> *years ago. "You still have four parents left to lose." We*
> *were startled and indignant. "Don't feel sorry for us,"*
> *Peter responded for us both. "We feel very fortunate*
> *to still have all four parents." She understood what the*
> *future would hold so much more than we did.*

Nothing has prepared me for what I am experiencing right now. Nothing could. For it is too complex and horrific to prepare for. Prior to living through it, I would have thought it unimaginable. But now, it is what dominates my time, my psyche, my energy, my life. Everything that is not this is trivial, insignificant. Because my inability to save my mother is the hardest thing I have ever had to face. And I'm sure that watching me try is one of the hardest things she has ever had to do.

Walk This Way

Visitors walk slowly as they approach a care facility. They typically carry a bag and walk with their heads down, shuffling slowly toward the door.

This is accentuated in caregivers. They are more tired and have more to carry, figuratively and literally.

Leaving the facility is different, however. Casual visitors walk at a clip and sometimes run. They are free; they are liberated. They served their time, did their good deed. They are so relieved to have it over with and so grateful to be able to leave. They can't get out of there fast enough.

Caregivers, however, know no such relief upon leaving. Our gait does not become lighter or more bouncy. We leave with the same heaviness we arrived with. And we carry stuff out – different stuff than we brought in. We are chronically tired, all the more so for realizing that tomorrow, we will walk this way again.

High Heels

I awake from an ether-induced stupor, alone in a cold, sterile facility. The pain in my throat tells me my tonsils have indeed been removed. I lie there waiting, not sure what will happen next. Still groggy from the anesthesia, I drift in and out of sleep. I am alone and scared. I am seven.

Then I hear her coming, hear her high heels clicking rapidly down the hall. I instantly know that is my mother. She breezes into my room like a breath of fresh air, exuding her typical high level of energy and self-confidence. She hugs me, and I can feel the excitement of her world of business and politics emanating from her professional garb. I know that she has postponed or interrupted something important to be with me, know that I am more important to her than any unfinished business. She strokes my head and gives me ginger ale until I drift back to sleep. But I can still hear the distant clicking of her high heels when she leaves.

Today, more than 40 years later, it is my high heels that click down a sterile hallway to where my 87-year-old mother now lies alone. It is she who awaits a visit, awaits someone to comfort her, to assuage her fears and loneliness. To give her a sip of water. I am the one who brings the sights and sounds of the outside world into her little room. And I am the one whose heels she hears getting fainter as I too soon leave her alone again.

"I heard you coming," she says as I enter her room tonight.

"I know you did, Mom, because I remember hearing you walking down the hall when I was in the hospital." I tell her the story of my recognizing the sound of her high heels after my tonsillectomy. She cries, and I cry. We cry for all the places she can never go again. We cry because our collective world has gotten so small. We cry because our time together is drawing to a close.

It is now my turn to take care of this woman, to pay on a debt I can never fully repay. It is I who must now miss meetings and appointments and parties because she needs me. For there are many places my high heels take me, but none as important as to my mother's bedside.

Others

Others can toilet her, wash her, dress her, feed her, kiss her and love her, which they do.

Others take very good care of her. But they cannot call her Mama and hear her say, "You are my baby." Only her family can share true intimacy with her, not borne of dependence but borne of a lifelong dedication to each other. Only her family can stroke her head in a way that says we are one.

Others take very good care of her, and I am very grateful. But I carry the duty and the privilege of her blood running through my veins. And the love I feel knows no bounds. She feels it too: "No one hugs me like you do," she says.

The kindest thing I can do for my mother is to just accept her as she is now. To not show my pain or disappointment but instead reflect back to her my total appreciation and support. I wonder if that's easier for Others to do – those who have no prior knowledge of her capabilities – than it is for loved ones who end up frustrated and disappointed by her decline.

Others serve a most important role in a way I had not contemplated before. I owe a great debt to Others.

Hair

She had always worn a hat for style. But after treatment, hats were used to mask that she had no hair. From form to function.

What does it matter what my hair looks like when I go to see my dying mother? I ponder as I primp in the mirror.

Yet, she always comments that my hair is pretty, although she can barely focus her eyes now. And she strokes it with her one working hand when she can reach it comfortably.

She would say hair is important, although she wouldn't have before last July when she began to lose her hair from the radiation treatments. Regrowing hair became a primary mission after that, an indication that her body was recovering.

"Is my hair growing back?" she'd ask. "Yes" was always my answer even when it wasn't yet.

But now it is. Her head is fuzzy with salt and pepper hair, sure to be as pretty as that she lost if given enough time. But time is a precious commodity these days.

My father strokes her fuzzy head and says, "Your hair is beautiful."

"Really?" she asks in disbelief, assuming he's making fun of her.

"Yes," he responds with conviction. One of the most supreme acts of kindness I have ever witnessed.

Normal

I tell her she looks great because she's sitting up straight. I tell her she's doing great because she opens her mouth for the spoon I hold. I tell her that her hair's growing back because a little peach fuzz has appeared. I cheer on every "good" bowel movement. I applaud every little twinge she thinks she feels in her leg or arm. I laud every minor sign that things are "normal," expanding and enhancing the observation to give her hope – us hope – that she is returning to "normal." That she is being restored, made whole.

For that is what she always did for me. She rationalized and twisted around any problem I had to make me come out on top. She was empowering for me, full of encouragement. So my cheerleader role in supporting her feels normal, although she will never again be.

Bizarre Ideas

Our blue parakeet is dying. He is all puffed up and panting. He has trouble getting to the higher perches and has stopped eating.

"We either have to get Mr. Bird to the vet or accept his impending death," I say to Peter. We agree to accept his death since there is so little that can be done for an old bird.

"Should we just let him go – let him fly away freely before he dies? He could have ten minutes of wonderful instead of a slow demise. Or should we just kill him now, put him out of his misery?"

Peter is taken aback. "Where are you getting these bizarre ideas?" he asks.

The answer is all too obvious. And I am not at all convinced that my ideas are "bizarre."

You Can Go Now

I make a quick stop home at lunch time and find Mr. Bird on the bottom of the cage. I pick him up, hold him, and feed him water from an eyedropper, which he eagerly drinks. I stroke his little blue head while he struggles to breathe.

I whisper to him, "You can go now. It's OK. You can go."

Within seconds, he closes his little round black eyes and dies in my hand.

They say nature gives us lessons when we are ready. In a matter of minutes, that bird has taught me how important it is to be present, to release a struggling body to the afterlife, to let go. And I witness the peace that comes over Mr. Bird once his struggle is over.

May I be able to be so generous in releasing my parents.

Mr. and Mrs. Bird were lifelong companions, and we expected her to die shortly after he did. She whimpered and ate less for a short time, but then resumed her routine and lived several more years. Another good lesson from nature about going on with your life after loss.

A Perfect Storm

I asked two months ago and was relieved when the answer was "no." But today the doctor calls to advise me that he is making a referral to Hospice for my mother.

A bittersweet outcome – support is coming because my mother has less than six months to live.

Appropriately it's raining. A cold hard downpour. The perfect weather in which to be told that my mother's time is drawing near, that no further medical interventions are called for.

As the doctor tells me on the phone, I watch myself in the mirror as if it were an out-of-body experience. Because sometimes, when the pain is so great, your body and spirit separate out of self-preservation.

I appear to take it well, the way my mother took it when the doctor told her that my father had less than two months to live. I graciously thank him and hang up.

Hospice calls me shortly thereafter to do an intake. The contact is light, casual, as I turn my mother's personal data over to an end-of-life agency. I even chomp on a sandwich, telling myself this is just routine, nothing has changed. The clock didn't start ticking just because we got a referral to Hospice...did it? After all, my dad "graduated out" of Hospice a few months before and is doing well.

For the rest of the day, it pours – inside and out.

How to Say Goodbye

What do you do when you're told time is short for someone you love? Do you try to make up for lost time by packing so much into the remaining time? Do you embark on a mission to see the world together, to do it all while you still can?

Or do you relish just being in her presence, content just to hear her breathing and sighing? Do you want her all to yourself, or are you willing to share her final hours?

Do you accept the diagnosis, or do you fight it? Do you express your grief openly, or do you put on a happy face? Do you pretend it won't really happen, or do you dwell on the impending loss?

In the final analysis, love shared is the only absolute when such questions are confronted. The experience of having loved and been loved is the only determinant as to how to say goodbye.

To Tell the Truth

"Are we going to be OK?" she asks, using the plural pronoun that signifies a recognition that our fates are now intertwined.

"We'll do the best we can every day, Mom. And eventually, it'll be OK."

"I'm trying to figure out where my head is going," she tells me. "I don't want to go berserk. And I don't want them to cut it open to see what's going on."

"They won't, Mom. We won't let them."

She smiles, a rare occurrence these days. "Good. Do you think I'm going to be all right?"

"Yes, Mom."

"How come?"

"Because whatever happens will be all right. God will take care of you."

"Do you worry about me, dolly?"

"No," I lie. Then I reconsider; there is no time like the present to tell the truth.

I change my answer: "Well, yes, Mom. I worry about you a lot."

"You do? What do you worry about?"

God, so many answers could be given. I could give her a litany of concerns. Fortunately, I find the truth and a way to say it at the same time.

"I worry that you are not content in your current situation," I respond.

"I'm content when you're here," she tells me. "And tomorrow we'll have more time together."

"Yes, we will. Goodnight."

Although I am fatigued, I feel privileged that I can be with her

during these final days. My love for her is the greatest truth I have
ever known.

Not Enough

My mother clings tightly to the hand of the Hospice nurse in
her room. She tells the nurse of the trauma she has gone through
with the radiation treatments, describing them in detail.

I am struck by how much my mother discloses during their
first visit. And then I hear her whisper, "I need more support. I
need more *outside* support. Do you know what I mean?"

I didn't see this coming – I never dreamed she'd be willing to
confide in a stranger. But it is now clear to me that she needs more
comfort than I can provide. She needs Hospice visitors to be able to
speak openly and honestly about her fears and feelings without worrying about upsetting her family. Try as I might, I am not enough.

Finding Peace

"I found great peace in your mother's presence today," Billy
tells me on the phone. "I just held her hand as she lay in bed. It
was so peaceful, I could have stayed all day."

Sadly, I do not find peace when I am there. I am tortured by
my self-imposed busy-ness. I am never at rest, so busy am I making everything "right."

When I visit her later, my mother's eyes are sparkling. She tells
me of her visit with Billy.

"He's a good soul," she says.

"He loves you very much," I tell her.

"I know he does. I love him too. He's a good kid."

Together today, they found peace. What a precious gift he gave
to both of us: A lesson in being present.

Fought Like a Tiger

I tell Billy that I am working on accepting my mother's inevitable fate, trying to find peace for both of us.

"I'm glad to hear that," he replies. "You fought like a tiger for her when there was still hope. Now it's time to start letting go."

Fought like a tiger. He's so right. I gave it everything I had. But it no longer makes sense to try to keep her alive, although that runs counter to my desire to hold on to her forever.

So how do I start letting go?

> *I still sometimes wonder if I did give it everything I had. Wasn't there something else I could have done?*

No Need

No need to set the alarm anymore; I can't sleep past dawn.
No need to push vitamins; there is no cure.
No need to wipe spills off her clothing; there'll be more.
No need to save anything for a future or better time; now is
    all we have.

A Good Day

Today I have two smiling parents.
They sit together and eat the food I made for them.
I have a chance to be present, to share memories.
All in all, a good day.

Yet I've learned that one good day does not a comeback make.
A good day doesn't even beget another good day.
A good day is simply one good day with no promise of
    anything beyond.
Let me just be grateful for this one good day.

A Bad Night

> *"I'm not sure I can do this,"* I lamented.
> *"You don't have a choice,"* Peter reminded me.

I can't take it tonight. Simply can't take it. Her crying, her simplicity, her repetitive movements, her leaning. It's all too much.

I am short with her, struggling to have patience. I snap at her a few times and feel like I can't do this anymore.

I can't stand the thought of going back tomorrow. I need a break. But how can I leave her alone?

A friend counsels that if something happens, I'll be better able to handle it after a break. If nothing happens, one day off won't matter.

I need a day off. Dare I take it?

Parallel Emotions

I don't go see either parent today. My work schedule does not permit it, but mostly I am too burned out to give them anything.

It's not unusual for me to go several days without seeing my father. But I did promise him I'd be there today. Yet I don't go; I can't go.

However, it's highly unusual for me not to see my mother. Our daily visits have been part of my routine for four months now. But not today. I can't go today.

My dereliction of duty brings forth both guilt and relief as parallel emotions. One does not override the other; they just weave in and out of my consciousness all night long. It doesn't feel good, and it doesn't feel bad. It just feels different.

Billy, Do You Know?

Billy, do you know she wasn't always like this?
Do you know that she was incredibly articulate and brilliant?
That she was quick in her head and on her feet?
That those green eyes sparkled and flashed with her ideas
      and insights?

Billy, do you know she had a sprightly walk?
Do you know she had a beautiful wardrobe and carried herself
      with such grace and dignity?
Do you know she was passionate for social justice and generous
      to charity?
Do you know her hair was so soft and full of curls, and her legs
      were perfectly shaped?
Do you know she had a beautiful smile?

Do you, Billy? Do you?
You can still see it, can't you?
You can imagine it beyond the illness that has kept her
      bedridden these many months.

Help me see it too.
Help me remember this incredible woman who was my mother.
Because I know there was no one else like her.

Showing Up

My mother's long-time friend and political ally calls to say he is coming from Rochester to see her.

"You're certainly welcome to come," I say hesitantly. "But I'm not sure you should see her like this. If I had a choice, I'd remember her as she used to be."

"I'm prepared," Ed says with conviction. "I'll always remember her as she was. But I'm her friend, and I want to see her as she is."

I'm afraid of what my mother's reaction might be to Ed coming, as she is a proud woman who doesn't like to be vulnerable. I don't believe she'll want Ed to see her in this debilitated state.

I am wrong; she is delighted to hear he is coming: "Let him come. It'll be good to see him. In fact, let anybody come who asks to see me."

That's what friendship is all about: Showing up. I wish more people would.

> *Ed died just a couple years later. Sadly, I didn't know he was ill so didn't go see him. I do show up at his grave on occasion, which is not far from my mother's.*

Still Beautiful

"Your mother is so beautiful," the aide tells me.

"Yes, she really was."

"No, I mean she is beautiful still…now. She is so beautiful."

"I'm glad you can still see it."

"It's still there," she declares.

The Transition

The transition has begun. There is nothing for me to carry in tonight. My mother has no material needs for me to meet. I feel I have lost my purpose. In reality, I may just be finding it.

From cure to care.
From hope to despair.
From holding on to letting go.

From managing to collapsing.
From my mother to a patient.
From hospital to Hospice.

Hold her hand instead of handing her water.
Hug her instead of feeding her.
Feed her spirit instead of her body.
For the body is leaving – the spirit will remain.

Part Five: Just Take Her

Just Take Her

*I used to recoil when my minister said, "Death came as
a friend" when announcing that someone had died after
a long-term illness. I now understand the context.*

Take her, I cry. Just take her! Don't let her suffer any more.

I plead with the heavens to end my mother's misery, to let
death come. Conversely, I beg God to heal her.

But to whom am I pleading? Is there a "god" out there? Is there
anyone who will listen, who could answer my prayers?

"It's not up to you," Peter reminds me. I know that. But who
else is there? It seems there is no deity watching or caring as my
prayers go unheeded day after day. Yet, curiously, I still pray –
hoping against hope someone will hear me...and take her. Or,
better yet, heal her.

To Heaven

*"Your mother is doing internal work," the Hospice
chaplain told me. "It's exhausting, but she's got to do it
to prepare herself for her journey."*

My mother often closes her eyes as if to escape when subjected to a gruesome reminder of her paralyzed state. When things get too tough, she goes inward with much dignity and grace.

She squeezes her eyes tightly shut and gives a little frown as if to say, *I'm not really here. This isn't happening to me. I could leave here if I tried hard enough.*

"Where do you go?" I ask her.

"When?"

"When you close your eyes like that."

"To heaven," she responds. "But not really."

Scheduling Death

> *"It's up to God now," so many people said. But I told my cousin Bobby that I think it's up to my mother. "Same difference," he responded. "The god within her will make that decision."*

"I think I should just die," my mother says.

"Do you really want to?" I ask.

"Yes, I pray every night that I will die."

"Should I pray that you die too?"

"That isn't necessary. I don't want to push it."

We both laugh.

"I believe you are strong enough, Mom, to be able to decide when you want to die and to make it happen."

"I believe that too. I'll give you some warning – maybe next week."

"I'll be ready when you're ready, Mom," I lie.

"OK, dolly. Thank you."

Dying is a Transitive Verb

*"It's just too bad this is taking so long," said Dorothy, my
mother's long time friend.*

You don't just go from being alive to being dead. You die. And
dying is a process – a difficult process, no matter how you die.

What is to be gained by the lingering and the suffering? Why
do we choose to put a quick end to our pets' suffering and let our
human loved ones gasp for air, choke, cry, groan, hurt? Where is
the glory in that? What is the benefit?

Offer it up, some fervent Christians tell me. *Jesus suffered for
our sins. We must now suffer.*

I don't buy that! My mother does not deserve to suffer.

Tragedy

*We don't know how it will end; we only know it
will end.*

As I look at the young adults disabled from car accidents in
my mother's ward, I try to put our situation in perspective: Is it a
tragedy when someone 87 years of age gets sick? In the scheme of
things, I guess it's not a tragedy. Since we all die eventually, and
my mother has lived to be 87, it's less of a tragedy and more of a
loss for us.

But then again, it's OUR tragedy. Tragedy is relative to the af-
flicted parties. There isn't an objective tragedy meter. Tragedy is
simply measured by the tears in the eyes of those affected.

I wish she were simply living an old person's life – a peaceful
slow existence. I wish she were not living with disease – especially
this disease. That said, this is a tragedy.

My dad ended up "living an old person's life." That was certainly no picnic either.

The Lost Weekend

Days slipped away as my parents slipped away.

The Sunday sun is setting. Two glorious days of beautiful weather, despite the advent of fall.

Yet I did not experience the sunshine. My weekend was given over to the care and feeding of my parents.

I am both proud of myself and resentful that my time and life are not my own. I know I am a good daughter. And in the end, that will be of great consolation. But right now, I am tired and wistful.

Holding On

Having even a piece of my mother – her warm cheeks, her soft hands, her green eyes – is better than losing her completely. I still have her to some extent. I still have a mother; I am still her child. I will cling to this while it is still available to me.

Yet, this is not the mother I knew. This period of time distorts her image and my memories. Her illness has stolen her from me. It is best that she physically leave as well so as to preserve her likeness in our hearts and minds. So she doesn't see the pity in our eyes, pity that would most assuredly destroy her as much as any disease ever could.

Flat

I am flat.
I am empty.
The garden is overgrown.
The leaves are starting to turn and fall.
My mother is slipping away.
And I am flat.

Is it because of the medication?
Or that my tear vial is all filled up?
Perhaps it is that I no longer will her to live if this is to be
    her life.
Whatever it is, I am flat.
Because there are worse things than losing your mother.
Much worse things. Like watching her suffer.

"I just want to die," she cries.
"I just want to die."
Then she is flat –
Because where do you find joy in your tiny nursing home
    room?
And what encouragement could I possibly offer?
I am flat.

Be Not Afraid

"I'm not afraid," she says. "I'm not afraid."
She is sobbing.
"You will go straight to heaven," I tell her. "You're an angel!"
"Don't talk silly," she says. "I'm not that good."
I tell her why I think she is "that good," all the things she has

done for others.

"You're already a saint," I say.

"Don't talk about your mother like that – it's blasphemy!"

I tell her how lucky I've been to have her, how we've had so many good years together.

"Don't cry for me," she says.

"I will, Mom. I will. I won't be able to help it."

"Then don't cry too much. I'll be watching over you always."

"I know you will," I respond.

> *Be not afraid. I go before you always.*
> *Come follow me. And I will give you rest.*
>> Hymn sent to her by her cousin Alex,
>> later engraved on her headstone

Prayers

"There are no atheists in foxholes," Chris told me.

"Do you pray for me, Patty?" she asks.

I answer yes, but I don't know. I think I used to but now feel abandoned by God since no good came of it. Instead, I rail, I cry, I scream, I write, I reflect, I curse. How does prayer differ from these activities? Doesn't it all just go off into the ether anyway?

"I never pray for myself. Never," my mother continues. "I always pray for you girls. In fact, I've always prayed that something would happen to me instead of to you girls." *Oh, dear.*

I reflect upon my own pleas for intercession and realize how central my own needs have been. Although my mother is of primary concern, my prayers have too often been for myself: *Help me...Don't take my mother.*

I will work on changing that, on presenting my mother's interests first to the Almighty. It is hard, but more noble and worthy. So while my mother won't pray for herself, I can do it for her.

Please, God,
Hold my mother in the palm of your hand and care for
her. Be merciful and compassionate toward this woman
of faith.

Your Father Fell

They call me at work: "Your father fell, but he wasn't hurt."

Flashbacks of the life-altering phone call from Florida. But now he is just down the road, so I rush over to see him. He is in pain.

Later that day, a fracture is detected; my father broke his other hip.

I have been so worried about my mother. Did my neglecting to worry about my father lead to his accident?

Pastoral Care

"My dad's having hip surgery tomorrow. Could you please say a few prayers with him tonight?"

It's 8 p.m. when I stick my head in the doorway of the Chaplain's Office to make this request. She leaves her desk and rises to greet me. Intuitively she asks, "How are *you* doing?"

I begin to sob. I tell her of the events of the last ten months, from my dad's first hip surgery to my mom's brain tumor. Sharon looks at me with compassion.

"Nothing is working out," I lament.

"It's working out," she responds, "Just not the way you want."

We talk about my faith journey. I tell her of my vacillation between believer and non-believer. She assures me that is normal at times like these, making it clear to me that she considers it important to believe but not judging my uncertainty.

She tells me to symbolically let it all go, let it drop from my hands. I can always pick it up again, she says, but I can also leave some of it on the ground if I choose.

"You can't do it all. You can't save them," she tells me.

I get a glimpse of serenity. The dark cloud lifts, if only temporarily. I thank Sharon for the talk, for recognizing that I am also in pain.

"See? God does provide," she says. "I was here tonight when you needed me."

"Happy" Birthday, Mom

My sister and Aunt Bertha came to celebrate what is likely to be my mother's last birthday. My father was in the hospital recovering from hip surgery.

"Happy" birthday, Mom. Today you turn 88. Seems like we should be grateful you had such a long life. But it still feels like it is being cut too short.

Heart and Soul

She told me she had no more tears left. But she did...

"You're so good, dolly," she tells me. "You've done so much for me."

She pauses and then asks, "Patty, do you feel sorry for me?"

I am unsure of the "right" answer so I decide that I owe her the truth.

"Yes," I solemnly reply. "I do."

She begins to cry: "I don't want you to feel sorry for me."

I can't tell if she doesn't want to inflict pain on me or if she doesn't want to be pitied.

"Don't cry for me," she says. I point out how much she herself cries.

"I know I should be braver," she says. "There's nothing stopping me from being brave."

"You're not ready to be brave yet. This is all happening so quickly," I tell her. "You'll be brave when you're ready."

"It's my soul," she sobs. "It's the difference between my heart and my soul."

I tell her that her soul is beautiful and that it is getting ready to leave her body. I tell her that her soul is going to a new, more beautiful place, after her heart gives up.

"I hope so," she replies. "I hope so."

My Dear Nurses

Knowing that reinforcement would be needed, two nurses come in together to see Peggy, my mother's 90-year-old roommate. True to form, she is ready for them.

"Peggy, we need to do a tuberculosis test on you."

"What for?"

"We do one annually on all our residents."

"Not on me, you don't."

"Yes, we did it last year. It's in our records."

"I don't think so. But even if you did, I don't want one this year."

"You really won't let us do it?"

"No."

"Do you want a hearing aid, Peggy?"

"No, I don't want one."

"Why not?"

"Because that's just one more thing someone will have to help me with."

"You haven't been eating very much, Peggy. Are you depressed?"

"No, I don't like the food here!"

"What's going on, Peggy? Have you given up?"

"My dear nurses. It is simply that I am already too old."

"Will you at least let us give you a flu shot? You would get very sick if you got the flu…"

"No, thank you. May I take a nap now?"

They respectfully oblige and leave. I then go to Peggy's bedside and tell her I admire her spunk and that she's right to follow her instincts.

"They probably think I'm crazy," she responds. "But I just don't want them doing all that stuff to me anymore!" She thanks me for the support, saying it's hard to know what to do when making decisions about your own health care.

I Hate Hospice

I hate having to be affiliated with Hospice. I hate having to attend meetings, knowing people at Hospice gatherings, being part of the Hospice "family."

I hate the new circles I necessarily run in, the way my "leisure time" is spent, the places I now go.

I hate feeling like a pathetic victim, so deserving of sympathy.

I hate Hospice.

But what would I do without it?

Angry at God

> *"You're the most religious person I know," I told my*
> *mother. "You pray a lot."*
> *"Well, it's worked so far, hasn't it?"*
> *No, I said to myself, it sure hasn't.*

"Miracles are possible," my Uncle Art keeps reminding me. But I'm afraid to believe that any longer. I can take no more disappointment. So my invocation to God for intercession has turned to anger this weekend.

My mother still believes she can be helped by her faith. I've been finding comfort in the power of the Almighty. But now I realize God isn't performing any miracles for us.

"Stop it," I scream aloud to the now non-existent deity. "You are mean and cruel to let her suffer like this. She believed in you. No self-respecting god would do this. At least, not a god I could worship!"

All I can conclude is that if there is a God, he doesn't care. And hence, it has become impossible for me to use the word *god* without adding the word *damn*.

Ready

I am ready to say goodbye; it's time for her to go. There is no more of my mother left. And what is in her place is taking me down with her – and I am letting it happen. I am eating poorly. I am not exercising or managing my stress well.

My real mother would not want this. The shell that remains is crippling me as well as her.

Part Six: Old Wounds

Old Wounds

> *"Your dad was a real man, and he ate quiche," she told me once with a twinkle. "But he ate hot dogs too so that balanced it out."*

"Your dad was a great basketball star," my father's 90-year-old college roommate told me in a recent phone call. "He was also an excellent soccer player. But even more memorable than the sports, your dad was a great dancer. And how the girls would squeal when he'd ask them to dance with him!"

I relay this story to my father in my mother's presence. "Neil always kept your secrets, didn't he, Nick?" my mother responds. More than 60 years after the fact, I detect both pride and jealousy.

Who Would You Save?

I'm racing out the door, late as usual. It's lunchtime, and both parents need me. I am again in the untenable position of deciding who needs me most right now. When I tend to one, the other is neglected.

My mother has "won out" since last June. Since her abilities are more limited than my father's now and her condition more medically dire, I tend to give her the lion's share of my attention.

Sadly, this situation has served to confirm my father's long held fear that his daughters love their mother more than they love him. My sister and I have dealt with his insecurities around his status our whole lives. It blatantly manifested in a game he used to play with us as children called "Who Would You Save?"

It would start out easy enough and fun even: "If Mr. and Mrs. Walsh were drowning, and you could only save one of them, who would you save?"

"Mrs. Walsh," I'd shout out with glee. What fun to be able to tell my dad indirectly which of his friends I liked better! To be able to decide who was worthy of my heroism. The next pair would then come up for rescue, and I'd determine their fate. The game proceeded through several of their accident-prone friends until…the ultimate question would eventually be asked: "If your mother and I were drowning, and you could only save one of us, who would you save?"

Oh my God! Why didn't I see this coming? Why did I participate in this stupid game again? It always ends like this!

My answer was always the same: "I'd save you both."

He'd persist: "You can only save one. Who would it be?"

"Both," I'd stubbornly respond. And then I'd leave the room, haunted by having been asked that question and by realizing that I could never tell him the truth.

Today I face this same forced-choice question as a reality, not as a game: *Which of my ailing, elderly parents will I save? To whose bedside shall I run when time is scarce? To whom shall I bring special food to entice them to eat? Whose hand shall I hold?*

I am beginning to understand that I can't save anyone, so the best answer to the question "Who will you save?" is neither. I will be present for each of them as they face their own figurative drownings. But I can only help my parents tread water for a short time until their next ship comes in. This I will do for both of them, with everything I have. And hope that someone will throw me a life preserver...quick.

Nothing to Miss

"I wish I would just die," my mother says. "You wouldn't miss me."

I am appalled. Day after day I am with her, caring for her. I ask her how she can say that to me.

"There's nothing to miss," she answers. "How could you miss this?"

I think to myself, *I will miss this. I just hope I don't remember this...*

In Your Little Book

As a writer herself, my mother had always been interested in my journaling. I would often find her looking at me as I wrote, and I would wonder if she knew I was writing of such things as my sadness over watching her age. For that reason, I write while she sleeps...and when I can't.

"Are you glad to be here, Patty? Do you like coming here?"

"I am delighted to be with you, Mom. I'm happy to be anywhere you are."

"Then write down in your little book that your mother is a pest, but you love her anyway."

"OK, Mom. I will."

We share a laugh.

I am Patty

I stopped calling myself "Patty" more than thirty years ago. I became "Pat" in ninth grade, reinventing myself as a sophisticated one-syllable-name teen – no longer Patty, which unfortunately rhymed with my physique as a child.

But my family and childhood friends continued to call me Patty, which I enjoyed although I never self-referenced as such outside the family.

Until now. Until my primary role as daughter was reinstated, having assumed responsibility for my parents' care. They call me Patty so, of course, their caregivers do. So now, when I am asked my name in the nursing homes, I reply, "Patty." I am Patty once again.

I find that comforting and reminiscent of simpler days gone by. Yet sometimes, I have to remind my own mother who I am: "I'm Patty, Mom." It both scares and embarrasses her that she sometimes cannot distinguish me from an aide. And it tears me apart to have to say those words to my own mother: I *am* Patty.

Stay Away From Me

Am I what she says I am, what she thinks I am? Is it possible she sees me more clearly than I see myself?

She says I am controlling, sick, in need of therapy. I suspect that's true, the only question lying in the definition of "sick." There are certainly days when I feel so fragile, likely to collapse under the weight of so many decisions. Yes, it seems I can accept those descriptors. But not as offered by her.

Her vitriolic message fills two voice mails. She uses my past confessions against me, intending to cut deep

She tells me never to call her again, to stay out of her life. There is a threatening tone to her message, and I am chilled by it.

"I guess I'll have to see you at our parents' funerals," my sister says. "But until then, stay away from me."

My sister and I later participated in a counseling session, where it became clear that we were playing out our parents' volatile relationship, both trying to fill the power void that our parents' illnesses created.

Boring

"He might have been a headache, but he never was a bore," my mom was oft heard to say about her husband.

"I love you."

"I love you, Nicky," she responds to her husband.

They sit in their respective wheelchairs with nothing more to say to each other, holding hands.

She smiles wistfully: "I think it was better when you used to yell at me. Now we're boring."

Jealousy

I am jealous of people with two healthy parents. I am jealous when I hear of a 95-year-old who is still vital. I feel cheated that maybe we could have had more years together. It happens. But not to us.

I am jealous of people who have not yet cared for an elderly parent so they have a spring in their step and laugh unencumbered.

I am even jealous that this isn't all behind me yet. And eventually, I will simply be jealous of people with *a* parent, healthy or not.

And no doubt, those who already lost their parents are jealous of me.

I now realize there is no point in being jealous of
anyone. We each take a turn at loss; we all experience
everything.

Not Very Old

"How old are you?" the priest asks my mother.

"I'm not very old, but I'm old enough to worry about my condition."

"What's old, Mom?" I ask.

"Ninety," her response. The priest chuckles.

When he leaves, she asks me, "Do you ever wet your pants?"

"No!" I respond, somewhat insulted. "Only very young and very old people wet their pants."

"Am I old?" she asks.

"Yes, Mom, you're old."

"Am I VERY old?"

"You're 88."

"Well, that's not very old," she says. "But I still might wet my pants if the aides don't get here soon!"

Harry Nilsson got it right: I'd rather be dead than wet
my bed.

Too Old to Dance

I have a chat with Charlie and then tell my mother that she and Charlie are the same age.

She looks at him and says, "That's too old."

"Too old for what, Mom?" I ask, embarrassed by her directness.

She continues to look at him. "Too old to dance," she says.

"And oh, how I used to love to do that," Charlie wistfully responds, as he slowly propels his wheelchair back to his room. He pauses halfway down the hall.

"I was quite good at it too," he says to no one in particular.

Instant Karma

"Are you ever lonesome because I'm in this place?"
"Yes, Mom. I miss you. Are you lonesome?"
"No, I have lots of friends here."

My mother was a controversial political figure most of her adult life. Like Cher or Madonna, Amelia didn't need a last name in our town (or beyond, for that matter). As the founder of a very effective taxpayer watchdog group in the 1960's, she had many detractors as well as fans. As her time draws to a close, she has remarked that a lot of people didn't care for her in our hometown. One thing for certain: No one was neutral about Amelia. They either loved her or hated her, making it tough to be her kid.

Not so anymore. Amelia will die among strangers who have become dear friends. She is deeply loved by all her caregivers who comfort and protect her. She will die with nothing but adoration and love from those nearest and closest to her.

My father, on the other hand, liked very few people back in the day. He was always jealous and competitive, leaving him with few friends. However, in his end time, he loves all. He waves to everyone and speaks to strangers. He will die having brought joy to so many others, when he had so selfishly kept it all for himself when he was younger.

In a similarly odd twist of fate, I now prefer to spend time with my father rather than with my mother. He is cheerful, animated, engaged and, perhaps most importantly, he is ambulatory.

This man I avoided much of my life, whom I was afraid to be alone with because of his dark side, has become my "favorite" parent. Has this evolved because it is too painful for me to see my mother as she is? Can I more easily accept my dad in a diminished state than the woman I adore? Both are disabled, but he is less so, making it easier for me to manage his care.

Perhaps you don't have to return for additional lifetimes for the karma to even out. Perhaps you can come full circle in one lifetime, learning the lessons before you pass over. Perhaps that is why we linger when quality of life seems to have left; we stick around for balance and reconciliation.

This time with my parents is proving to be so profound.

A Four Wheelchair Thanksgiving

All four of our parents come to Thanksgiving dinner – in wheelchairs. They are unable to roam freely around the house; they can only go where we take them.

How did it come to be that of all four parents, my mother would emerge as the weakest? My mother with so much pep and so engaging in the past is the most incoherent and incompetent of them all today. Seeing her in the context of the nursing home protects me from the comparisons that today seem so stark in my home.

I want to give thanks today...I just can't find a reason to do so. It is undoubtedly our last Thanksgiving together. Yet I am too numb to cry.

It would be a two wheelchair Easter.

Denial

> *"Everyone just keeps pushing me around," she told the*
> *aide. "I know I could walk if they just let me try. I could*
> *walk right out of here!"*

If we had it to do over, we might have been totally honest with her about the diagnosis and prognosis. Knowing the tumor is malignant might have enabled her to make an informed decision about the way she lives and dies. It might have helped her get her head together (so to speak) over her disability, rather than causing her confusion over not getting better as she fully expects. Our well-intentioned deception seems to be standing in the way of her reconciliation to her eventual fate.

Yet we did it for her – to keep hope alive for as long as possible, to aid in the possibility that treatment might work. After all, when she was told my father had only two months to live, she forbade the doctor and everyone else to tell him. Ten months later, he is more alive than she.

But the lie seems to have overshadowed the potential for acceptance. And what if it is continuing to perpetuate a life that should have ended before quality deteriorates too much?

We've tried to tell her the truth since, but her capacity for denial is quite well developed. She interpreted "There is no further treatment for your condition" as "You don't need further treatment." She cannot or will not hear the harsh reality, perhaps because we still couch it so carefully.

Which, upon this writing, makes me realize how finely tuned her defense and denial mechanisms always were. And now, she continues to selectively assimilate information and let go that which does not fit her paradigm. While I regret keeping information from her, this very assertive woman does not go seeking it either. Even after that doctor blurted it out to his medical students in front of her.

Jane, a Hospice nurse, tells me, "You die the way you live. If you practiced denial successfully in your life, you will keep it up when faced with death." So perhaps it's been up to her all along. She was no doubt astute enough when this began to pick up the incongruities. It seems we all chose to bury our heads in the sand in order to keep going.

My Flesh and Blood

As I leave my father's nursing home, I see her walking toward me in the parking lot. I don't recognize her immediately, so out of context she. But then I realize it is my sister, my flesh and blood, the only one losing the same two parents as I am.

I didn't even know she was in town.

We greet each other awkwardly, surprised by and uncomfortable with the unexpected encounter. We have a few brief moments as I walk her in; I then leave her to visit with my father – her father.

The walk back to my car seems to take an eternity. Tears stream down my face. At a time when we need each other the most, we have never been so far apart.

Part Seven: She Sleeps

She Sleeps

I watch her face – a face I have loved for more than fifty years – as she sleeps. She does not awaken when I call out, "Mama?" There is no sign that she can hear me or is aware of my presence. She sleeps.

I kiss her cheeks and her forehead. I stroke her head. I whisper in her ear, "I love you, Mama. It's OK to leave if you want. I'll be OK." But there is no acknowledgement.

She sleeps; I weep.

How foolish I am, I chastise myself. *How foolish to keep believing this could all work out.* "You never know," people tell me. But you do know – you just can't admit it or accept it yet.

She looks peaceful, content. For what do I wish? That she will open those beautiful green eyes once again, only to have them filled with tears at her plight? Or do I wish they would stay closed forever and she go to a better place? A little of both, I imagine. It seems counterintuitive to not wish for more life. Yet it seems selfish and cruel to do so.

As I leave her, I say aloud, "Goodnight, Mama. I love you."

"Goodnight, dolly. I love you," she responds with her eyes

still closed.

Although surprised that she responds, I treasure the reciprocal communication – both spoken and unspoken.

All Mixed Up

She is sound asleep in her wheelchair, slumped to one side. I stroke her head and face, and whisper words of comfort to her. But there is no response.

When I whisper, "I love you, Mom. I would do anything for you," her eyes suddenly open.

"I love you too, dolly. I would do anything for you too."

"Are you comfortable, Mom?"

"Yes, don't worry about me."

"Don't worry about me either, Mom. I'll be OK."

"We always worry about each other. You've had such a big job taking care of me."

"Have you had good care?"

"Yes, everyone has been great. Is your dad well cared for?"

"Yes, Mom, he is."

"Poor little guy."

"Don't worry about him either, Mom. He's OK."

"Everything got all mixed up, didn't it?"

"Yes, it did."

"Then I got all mixed up too, didn't I?"

"You got sick, Mom. You couldn't help that."

"You're still my baby," she replies, "But I'm not your mother completely anymore."

An odd phrasing but sadly true. Much of my mother is gone. But I can still physically be with this woman who gave me life.

She closes her eyes, and we say goodnight. And it was a good night, salvaged by one dangling conversation.

God Bless You

It always bugged me. Ever since I was a child, whenever I sneezed in my mother's presence, she responded in a worried voice, "Are you getting a cold?"

"No, Ma. Sheesh…C'mon, it was just a sneeze," I'd say in an irritated tone. I even hated sneezing in her presence because I knew the question I'd invariably hear. And her vigilance persisted into my adulthood without fail. Until now.

Tonight I sneeze in front of my mother, and she is silent. She opens her eyes to look at me but is silent.

How can she sit there silent in her wheelchair after I sneeze? Why doesn't she ask me if I'm getting a cold?

Ask me, Mama. Ask me! Because I might be getting a cold, and I want you to know, to care. I want to hear the question again from you.

Take Charge, Mom!

She was always in charge, in control. She was strong and powerful. She could make things happen and did. We believed she could even determine her own fate.

"I don't have a brain tumor," she told us definitively when the first tentative diagnosis came through. "I just had a little stroke, that's all."

So that was that. We believed it because she said so. If she said she didn't have a brain tumor, she didn't. End of story.

We lived with her proclamation for months, believing it when she said nothing would happen to her. We know now that we should not have accepted her self-diagnosis. Yet we wanted to believe she was OK. Perhaps more importantly, we wanted to continue believing in her infallibility. Losing both illusions would have been too hard.

And still today, I expect her to be proven right: this isn't really a terminal brain tumor. Although she lies half-paralyzed in her bed, I still expect her to take charge, to begin telling me how to get us out of this mess. I want her to reprimand me for making such a big deal out of her condition and for treating her like she's ill.

I want Amelia to be in charge again – of her life, of my life, of the world as she knows it. Because it's too hard when her influence is absent.

Take charge, Mom! Make it all be OK like it was before.

Amelia is no longer able to make it all be OK. I am on my own and so scared. Yet I still believe she just might rally…and I just want her back.

I just want her back.

C'mon, Mom

"C'mon, Mom. Raise your head."

"Chew your food. Swallow, Mom."

"Mom, you're drooling. You're making a mess."

Mom, please stop! Snap out of it. This isn't you! Be like you were. Don't make us go through this!

It would be better if you died – for both of us. Because I don't want to be angry, hurt, sad and scared anymore. And I don't want you to know that I am.

But I am scared, Mom. I am. And this time, you can't help me.

Maybe

> *My mother always said that pneumonia was "the old man's friend." Might it be "the old woman's friend" as well?*

Another bout with pneumonia. A tough rap to beat after what she's already been through. The realization that my best isn't good enough, that I can't save her no matter what. The feeling that my efforts were in vain and that they were even foolish. I am once again forced to face reality.

But maybe, just maybe…some vitamin A and garlic will knock this infection out of her. Maybe it's possible.

How will I know when it's really time to give up? Can you ever give up when you love someone this much?

> *My mother conquered the pneumonia against the odds. And I caught another glimpse that maybe we'd beat this brain tumor, maybe the radiation was just slow to kick in, maybe all those prayers…maybe.*

Hard Times are Over

Life had become so hard for my mother. Not just since she got sick but years before that. Her neighbors freely tell me that now. Why hadn't I been more aware of her struggle?

Tonight I tell her it'll all get better; it won't be so hard once we get through "this part."

She sleeps as I make these promises. *Make it come true,* I beg the heavens.

Two Twin Beds

My parents each have their own single bed in two different institutions. They each sleep alone now, after 62 years of marriage.

Their two wheelchairs also keep them apart. Even when they are together, the metal encasements make physical contact nearly impossible.

As my father and I are getting ready to leave her today, she asks him, "Which side of the bed do you want to sleep on tonight? Over there or over here?" she asks, pointing to the two sides.

Before my father can respond, the nurse hoists her into her twin bed.

"It's so sad, isn't it, Patty?" she says tearfully. And I can't help but concur.

My father is not to be deterred. He notices the folded cot in the corner that I have put there for the time when a round-the-clock vigil will become necessary.

"Who sleeps there?" he asks.

"No one," I respond.

"Then can I?"

"No, it's just being stored there," I lie.

"Then they should put it somewhere else," he loudly announces. And then turning to his wife, he gently says, "Someday you can come and live with me."

I then drive him back to his own little room and his own little bed.

Night Visitors

I hear a commotion down the hall. I think I recognize my father's voice, but I am too groggy to zero in on it. It's dark, except for the bright lights outside the door.

The voices become clearer. My father is arguing with the nurse, saying he wants to see his daughter, his daughter who is in the hospital following a tonsillectomy. I hear him say that he couldn't sleep so he brought my stuffed bear for me.

He sounds angry, and I register embarrassment that my father is raising his voice at the people taking care of me. The nurse, however, is insistent that he can't just barge in after visiting hours and that he should come back tomorrow morning. I hear some slamming and then silence. Slamming – just like home.

The nurse quietly enters my room and puts the bear in my bed. When she leaves, I grab for it and snuggle it. It's not just any bear – it's the bear my dad bought me after my mom dragged me away from it in the store, telling me it was too expensive. A few months later, I had found it on Christmas morning in the bottom of a big empty box "from Santa."

Today, I am the one going to see my father after visiting hours. After spending the evening with my mother, his room is a stop on the way home. He too is often sleeping when I sneak in the employee entrance, but nurses today know it's better medicine to get a goodnight kiss from a loved one than to toss and turn in a fist-clenched sleep. I try to bring him special treats that I hope he'll enjoy. And I can't help but note that I too have sounded angry at his caregivers from time to time in my zeal to protect him.

The circle remains unbroken. And the night is a little less dark thanks to night visitors.

I still have that bear but no longer my father. Isn't it incredible that the things we have outlast the people we love?

Cards Unopened

Cards were fun to get when this first began – so full of hope and get well wishes. Both the printed and the written words seemed to inspire and bring familiarity to my parents. How nice to be remembered!

But as my mother's condition worsens – the prognosis more dire – the cards seem a mockery. The incantations to "get better" seem almost cruel, a denial of the severity of the situation. I still read them aloud to her, but with a great deal of sadness. I skip over news from her peers about their travels and adventures. I skip over messages that are either too hopeful or too realistic. I edit and sugarcoat the words.

Not only can she not read them herself, she can't even open them. In my mind's eye, they represent one more loss. They have become a psychological burden, demanding action, a response.

So now they lie unopened in my house, in my car, in her room. It's not that the thought isn't appreciated, for it surely is. It's just that Hallmark cannot ease the pain of loss that has permeated our lives.

> I've spent so much time in the past trying to select
> cards with the "perfect" messages for others. Words do
> matter, but only the recipient can accurately assess the
> appropriateness.

Frustration

"Open your mouth, Mom! Open your mouth!"

My frustration mounts as the simplest of commands seems to stymie her. Why doesn't she just open her mouth?

What I refuse to accept is that she doesn't want to eat, despite my continued desperation to sustain her.

"Mom, why can't you do that?" I ask her exasperated. She laughs. For what else is there for her to do when asked such a ridiculous question?

Compared to what she is enduring, I have no right to be frustrated.

A Solitary Journey

"I'll take care of you, Mom," I promised.
"I'll take care of you too, dolly," she weakly replied.

"You just have to get to the point where it's OK that your mother won't eat. You have to accept that," Peter says.

It's so easy to give such advice when it's not your mother. So easily that assessment can roll off someone's tongue when he is not the one fearful that this nourishment may be the only thing standing in between life and death.

But they don't know how you are feeling – they couldn't possibly know. Because this is a solitary journey that both the dying person and the caregiver must take independently from each other and from all others.

You got to walk that lonesome valley.
You got to walk it by yourself.
Oh, nobody else can walk it for you.
You got to walk it for yourself.
                    -unknown

I Hate Her Today

My anger and disappointment overwhelm me today. I hate what she has become. I hate having to witness her descent into a non-functioning human being. I hate that she could not protect me from the deepest pain I have ever known, and is, in fact, the source of it.

I hate her irrational behaviors. I hate my mother today.

But it is not really her that I hate – because this is not my mother. My mother left me months ago. This is just another nursing home resident who acts bizarre and doesn't know what's going on. She just happens to look somewhat like my mother.

Should she die while I bear these feelings, I will have a lifetime of regret. But today, I hate her. Or maybe I just hate myself.

Not Like This

I want to believe that I won't remember her like this. I want to believe that I'll be able to shake these visual and auditory images and remember her as she was most of her life, not what she is at the end. I want to believe that I'll get over this trauma and eventually celebrate her life.

Because now we live under a cloud of grief and death. Death will come only after she deteriorates until she can function no more. The images will get worse until she is silent and still. And then I will be left with only memories. But of what?

Please don't let me remember her like this. Please.

At her wake, relatives and friends helped me remember her as she was.

All I Wanted

All I wanted was for her to have one more chance to lead a normal life. I so hoped after the radiation treatments ended, she'd have a window – no matter how short – where she would rally and be the woman she always was. That she'd move to my house and walk again. That I'd see that head thrown back in laughter, see her charm and grace again, if only for a short time. If only for one day.

I just wanted to see some benefit from the radiation she endured. I just wanted a miracle. And despite all my talk of letting go, I believed it possible up until now.

Now all I want is for her to be made whole again the next place she goes.

What does *she* want? I pray that her prayers will be answered.

> *God of compassion.*
> *Be with her this day.*
> *Fulfill her wishes.*

Be Grateful

> She is not in pain.
> She is comfortable.
> She sleeps peacefully.
> She is in a nice setting.
> I had her for so long.
> We had such a special bond.
> She loves me.
> And I love her.
> And we both know it.
> Be grateful.

While I Still Can

> I will hold her,
> touch her face,
> whisper in her ear,

hold her hand,
stroke her head,
reassure her,
while I still can.
For too soon, I will only be able to love her from afar.

Yet… maybe she doesn't want all this affection. She sometimes turns her head away from us and scowls when kissed or touched. My father takes that as rejection. Perhaps I do too.

I am reminded that she is doing her "internal work," beginning the separation process. It is so difficult to witness but so important to just let her be. Although she doesn't always speak, on occasion she nods or shakes her head. And sometimes she turns her head to rest against mine.

It's About MY Mother

I leave my mother's room crying tonight, and an aide asks me what's wrong. I tell her my mother is not doing well. She says, "I understand. I just went through that with my mother."

What do you mean your mother? We're the ones going through this, feeling this incredible pain. How could you possibly be hurting too? This is all about MY mother!

I am troubled, but I don't understand why. Did the aide diminish my seemingly unique situation and resulting martyrdom, or help me realize the universality of grief and loss? It's amazing how myopic we can become.

> *I was not the first person to lose my mother.*
> *It only felt like I was.*

December

The calendar reads December. But that can't be! How did we get to December? Where have the days gone? Days just fly by in this misty, seamless bog of angst and anticipation. Just like for my parents, the days and dates no longer matter to me, as one blends into another.

And how did it get to be the Christmas season? It seems time should have stood still, as our way of life screeched to a halt. Christmas has no right to arrive. It has no place here – there is nothing for it to do. There is no way to accommodate Christmas under these circumstances.

Come Summer

"I'll never be the same after this," I told Debby. "You're not supposed to be," she responded. "Every experience changes us."

Come summer, I'll be rid of all this responsibility.
Come summer, I won't have these worries.
Come summer, I can focus on me.

Come summer, it will all be OK.
Come summer, the stress lines will disappear from my face.
But...come summer, I won't have a mother.

How will I endure next summer?

Part Eight: When a Mother Leaves

When a Mother Leaves

> *"They say we choose our mothers before we are*
> *reincarnated," I told her. "And I chose you." To my*
> *surprise, my Catholic mother who did not believe in*
> *reincarnation answered, "I know. You were floating*
> *around out there, and I couldn't catch you."*

"Will you miss me?" my mother inquires, staring into my face.

I don't know whether we are talking about tonight or forever. But I sense it is a double entendre for my mother, again testing the waters. How can I display the right amount of pain – enough to show her how much I love her and not so much that she feels she must stay for me?

"I will miss you," I respond. "But I'll be OK."

"You will?"

"Yes, I will. You can leave me any time you want, and I'll be OK. I'll miss you every day, but I'll make it."

"I don't want you to remember me too much," she tells me. "If you remember me too much, you'll be very sad. I don't want you to be sad."

I can't hold back the tears.

"See? I can't leave you," she says.

"You must," I tell her sternly. "All mothers eventually leave their daughters, just like your mother left you."

"Yes, but I didn't handle it well when my mother left me. I don't want you to go through that."

"We all go through it, Mom. You can leave me."

"I don't want to leave you. You're my baby. I'll never leave you mentally," she promises. "I'm inside you."

"I'll never leave you either, Mom."

"Look at our tears running down your face," she astutely remarks. For we are once again one being.

The Perfect Mother

> *How can I curse the last few months when I had 50 years of the perfect mother for me?*

"You were the perfect mother for me," I tell her, painfully aware that I am already speaking in past tense.

"Then in your little book, tell them I was the perfect mother who messed up your life."

"You didn't, Mom."

"Yes I did, dolly. I did."

A Different Kind of OK

> *"She will definitely be OK," Marie said. "And so will you."*

My mother again laments, "I wish I were stronger. I'm not very brave."

I tell her she is an amazing woman, that she has always been so brave and strong. I also ask the question that has remained unspoken yet is always on the tip of my tongue: "Would you like me to do something to speed this up?"

She looks at me intently and is silent for awhile, as I hold my breath. "I wouldn't ask that of you," she responds. "You'd get in trouble for helping me, and I can't put my daughter in that position."

I cowardly fall silent, as I too am afraid of the act itself and the consequences. Yet what if she had accepted my half-hearted offer? Was I really prepared to "help?"

She tells me she is worried about me and asks, "Are we going to be OK?" With tears in my eyes, I tell her, "Yes, we will be OK. It's just a different kind of OK than we're used to."

Becoming

> We lay on the bed, side by side, four feet sticking out the bottom of the sheets. "Look!" she said excitedly. "My toes are wiggling. The radiation's finally starting to work!" I hesitated too long before explaining.

Her hands become my hands.
Her feet, my feet.
Her skin, my skin.
Her hair, my hair.

Her bones become my bones.
Her organs, my organs.
Her blood, my blood.
Her heart, my heart.

Her thoughts become my thoughts.
Her fears, my fears.

Her work, my work.
Her life, my life.

Her death, my death.

On Her Way

*"You and I both knew this day would come," Billy told
me. He was right, of course. But denial was pretty
effective.*

I recognize it – the advent of death. It looks and feels different from other scares we have had. She is disengaging from me,
refusing food, and staring into space. She is leaving.

The Hospice chaplain says my mother has started her journey:
"She's in a hammock resting comfortably between her earthly
caregivers and God. She has nothing more to do but wait to pass
over."

The doctor tells me she is "shutting down," starting the process
of dying. I can tell that without a medical degree. I know it because she is my beloved mother.

When asked if death is imminent, he responds, "If ten days is
imminent, then yes, it is."

Suddenly, we are in a countdown.

*My mom asked this doctor if she could hug him; he
readily consented and hugged her back.*

Mom, It's My Birthday!

"Mom, it's Kathy. It's my birthday. Pick up the phone, Mom.
Mom! It's Kathy. And today's my birthday! Mom? Mom?"

Her voice gets more and more desperate as recorded on the

answering machine. Fifty-seven years ago today, her mother gave birth to her. Today, her mother cannot even answer the telephone. She is dying in a small room with an answering machine.

The woman who gave us both life is dying. Our umbilical cords are being severed one more time as our mother is reborn into her next life, and we are forced to continue our lives without our source of sustenance.

But somehow I believe she knows it's her first born's birthday. *Happy birthday, dolly*, she says deep within her soul. *Happy birthday to my dear daughter.*

Ten Days

Is ten days a long time or a short time when your mother is suffering the agony of death, and you are powerless to keep her or to set her free? Will the days drag on, seeming like forever? Will I be wishing the time away, just wanting to get through it? Or will the days speed by, with too rapid a countdown, with every 24 hours bringing me closer to a loss that I will forever bear?

Ten more dinners, ten more visits, ten more, ten more. Or maybe only three or one. "Things can happen very quickly at this stage," they tell me; they may not even have time to call me.

Time takes on a whole new meaning. It is everything and nothing in the face of death. And after death, it is rendered powerless.

Christmas was nine days away.

Are You OK?

"You're OK," Billy told me. "You just don't think you are."

"Are you OK?"

Such a common, simple question becomes an imponderable in this context. For what could "OK" feel like after being told your mother is going to die within ten days?

So This is How it Feels

"I feel like I'm watching myself die," I told Jackie.
"You probably are," she responded. "A part of you is dying so that you can be re-born to a life without your mother."

Warm tears run down my cheeks onto my sweater. I have never been so alone. I am flat – nothing can arouse my interest. My stomach is turned inside out. My heart is palpitating. My joints ache. My eyelids are heavy; I look but cannot focus on anything.

I can imagine that the above is probably what my mother would have written too if she could, proving that a part of me is truly dying with her.

Is This the Day?

Each morning upon waking, I wonder to myself: *Is this the day? Is this the day I lose my mother?*

Which day will forever leave a black mark on the calendar and on my heart, I wonder?

I hope not today – I'm still not ready. But I suspect I never will be.

Fear

*"You'll still have her," Marie told me. "You won't have
her physically, but you will feel her presence even more
than you do now."*

"What are you most worried about?" the Hospice social worker asks me.

The answer comes easily: "I'm afraid of not having her physical presence. Of not being able to feel her warm cheeks, hold her
hand, or hear her voice."

I continue: "I'm also afraid of my life without her. What will I
do with the time?"

How ironic that I sometimes resented spending so much
time caring for her. And now, her hats, her smell, her noises, her
breathing, her tears – I will miss them all.

Dear Mom II

*She did not wake during my visit, except to give a sweet
smile and say, "Hi, dolly," before drifting so peacefully
back to sleep. So I read her this letter I wrote yesterday.
I know that she heard me although she did not
acknowledge it.*

Dear Mom,

*I want to tell you so much, to share so much with
you. But you are gone from me.*

*This is the end. We are out of rabbits to pull from
the hat. And while it feels like defeat, I want us both to
feel like we gave it our best shot. Because we did, Mom.*

*None of us knows how we will go. I so wish it were
different for you. But you made it to 88, a gift for which*

I am trying to give thanks.

I am so very grateful to you for who and what I am.
You leave behind an incredible legacy of social justice,
public service, activism and advocacy. I will carry on
because of the lessons you demonstrated.

I know you will continue to watch over me and that
I will continue to feel your considerable influence over
me and over the earth. We are better people for having
had you here.

Godspeed, Mama.

Love,
Patty

Seeking Reassurance

I seek reassurance from her that I did right.
I want her to think me a good daughter,
Despite the disappointment I feel in myself tonight.
She is silent.
She yawns, eyes closed,
As I unfairly use her as my confessor.

I sob openly in front of her.
Heaving, gasping for breath.
I cover my face with my hands, overcome with despair.
She makes no move to comfort me.
She does not see or hear her daughter.

Nothing feels as lonesome as crying in front of your mother.
With no hint that she knows or cares.

The Source

As the reality of her impending death hits, I crumble in despair. I sob and thrash, so desperate to feel better. I then think of a solution: *I'll call my mother! She'll make me feel better.* But wait – she is the source of my excruciating pain. She is the one making me hurt this badly. It is her sickness that has gone wrong in my life. Her disability and inability to conquer it pains me in a way I thought unimaginable just a few short months ago.

Irony I could do without.

She Doesn't Know

Had she known, my very overprotective mother would never have allowed me to do many of the things I've done these last several months. She doesn't know that I drove in snowstorms and ice storms to see her. That I walked alone through dark hospital parking lots to get to my car, that I drove alone through "the bad part of town" late at night. That I frequently stayed overnight at a friend's house because I was too tired to drive 40 minutes home. That I threw my back out lifting her wheelchair. That I started taking anti-depressants and sleeping pills. That I ate junk food on the run. That I badgered her doctors. That I was exhausted all the time and cried myself to sleep. That I missed work frequently.

She would die – literally and figuratively – if she knew I had done all these things in service to her. She would never have wanted me to suffer so much loss and pain. Yet she unintentionally made me more vulnerable than I've ever been.

Lucky for both of us, she doesn't know.

I Dream of Her Whole

She is walking.

She is talking.
We are sharing experiences, going places.
Every night.

Every night, I dream of her whole.
I wake up only to have reality hit me in the face.
She's not whole; she's broken.
Or is she?

It takes a while for my fantasy to fade each morning.
It seems so real.
Is it a longing for the past, for what was?
Or does it herald that she will be made whole in her next
   life?

I don't know.
I only know that instead of being disappointing and disturb-
   ing,
The image of my mother whole is quite satisfying and com-
   forting.
For while I dream of her whole at night,
I still love her just as much by day.

No Words Left Unspoken

"Sometimes it's hard to fully express myself," she says.
"What else do you want to say, Mama?"
"I love you."
"I know."
"I had two wonderful daughters."
"And we had a wonderful mother. I think I've said it all. Except

thank you."

"You're welcome, dolly."

"Is there anything else you'd like to say, Mama?"

"No."

Such a Long Journey

As I tearfully said these words to her, she slept. But periodically she asked, "What?"

"It's been such a long journey, Mama.
Such a hard journey we have taken.
We didn't know it would be this hard.
But we really didn't have a choice.
I'm glad I was on the journey with you.
But I am tired now as are you.
It's time for our journey to end.

I'm glad we were together, Mama.
Even though we didn't know where we were going.
We still had each other.
On this long, long journey."

A Merry Little Christmas

My parents sit together at the holiday party at her nursing home. Dad – the bell of the ball – and Mom silently watching his antics. I sit between them, facilitating the feeding process and interpreting events for each.

It is their 62nd Christmas Eve together as a married couple, undoubtedly their last. And it is my first Christmas with my parents in over two decades since they had always traveled to Florida before the snow hit.

No, it's not what I would have wished for, nor they. But I can spend Christmas with them once again, and let the promise of joy and good things to come wash over us.

Two failing parents have actually heightened my awareness of the holiday and the magic (or diversion) it can bring. Surprisingly, here I am singing Christmas carols during the saddest of any Christmas I've ever experienced. For me, it is my truest Christmas – the Christmas most representative of what Jesus was born to teach and do. It is not fun or glitzy – but it is a true tribute to the one we honor on the holiest of days.

> *On the way back from the Christmas party, I tried to prepare my father for the inevitable: "How do you think Mom is doing?" "Good!" he responded with enthusiasm, wishing it so.*

The First Christmas...the Last Christmas

My father gets to sit at the head of the table again this Christmas. Only the table is in the family room of his nursing home. And the "head" of the table is the only place his wheelchair will fit. And for the first Christmas in 62 years, his wife isn't by his side. But he dons his Santa Claus hat, smiles and eats, never once asking for her.

He cries when he realizes we have gifts for him, and he has nothing to give us in return. He leafs page by page through the dog book I give him, stroking the photos. Peter and I leave him at 11:30a.m. to spend the rest of his Christmas day alone, as we go on to see my mother.

Christmas does not exist for her this year. I give her no presents, as she is unable to open them with only one functioning hand. Her pureed meal is the holiday feast.

I cannot even bring myself to utter the words "Merry Christmas" to her.

"Happy" New Year

"I'm such a sleepy head," my mother's roommate tells me. "I think I just need some fresh air. It's so awful being in bed all the time – I have to snap out of it! So does your mother. Perhaps things will be better in the new year."

I give her a hug: "Perhaps they will, Peggy."

"Happy New Year," I say to my mother half-heartedly.

"Happy New Year," she softly echoes.

Happy indeed...

Not Ready to Leave

> "I'm losing my mother," I told Elsie, another nursing
> home resident. "Again?" she said. "You were just losing
> her a few weeks ago." To my surprise, I laughed out
> loud. And so did she. You do get what you need, even if
> you don't know you need it.

Twenty days and counting since the doctor advised me of the ten-day window until my mother's passing. He admits that while he has medical evidence to draw on, he doesn't know what will drive or motivate her departure.

She just isn't ready yet. Perhaps she's hanging on for one more visit from my dad or my sister. Or perhaps I'm holding her back because she knows how bonded I am.

Tonight while coughing and choking, she says, "I can't stand this," a stronger statement than I've heard previously.

"It's so hard, isn't it, Mom?"

"What's hard?"

"Being so sick."

"No, it's not so hard," she responds looking surprisingly at peace. "I'm OK."

She's still not ready to leave.

"Ten days" turned out to be 46 days. Bernie Siegel was right – no one can predict how long someone will live.

From This Wheelchair

Lucy asks about my mother, and I tell her she will be leaving us soon. Lucy, whose grandmotherly face and kind soul I have loved since my mother and I arrived at this place. Lucy, who always seems to be concerned about everyone. Lucy, who sits quietly and reads her Bible.

"It's time," I tell Lucy.

"I understand," Lucy replies. "I wish I would go too. I'm no good to anyone. I can't even go to the bathroom by myself. I've buried two sons already and my third is ill. What's the point of my staying alive?"

I tell her she does still have a purpose, that her kindness has helped me through my mother's illness.

"Thank you," she says. "I used to work in a nursing home, you know. I was so busy there that I didn't see the people – I mean *really* see the people. But I see them now. I can see all their pain and suffering from this wheelchair. Because that's all I have to do now – watch from this chair."

She continues: "I pray for all these people every night. Because I see their pain now. I didn't see it then."

Part Nine: Just Passing Through

Just Passing Through

> "Are you upset that we've spent so much time in this
> place?"
> "Yes, Mom. I am."
> "How come?"
> "Because I didn't want the end to be like this for you."

"We won't be staying here long, Mama. Just until you complete rehab. Then we'll be going home," I had told her when we first arrived at this facility.

"Do you really think I'll be going back home with you?" she would periodically ask, eyes full of hope.

"Yes," I always answered. "We have your apartment all set up for you." And we did. For months, her belongings waited for her return in an apartment adjoining our home.

We didn't know it would end like this when we brought her to Albany last June. That the ride from the airport would be her last ride with family in a car. So full of hope were we that we could beat this.

Now I clean out the room, sorting her limited possessions into piles. Some to the trash, some to residents, some to staff, some to goodwill, some to home. Taking it all away because we're leaving soon…just like I had told her.

Please Get in Touch With Us

It is clear that she is taking her last few breaths. We hold her hands, stroke her head, and give her permission to leave us.

"We'll be OK," we say, although the tears streaming down our faces belie such reassurance. "It's OK to go now."

The doctor and alarms from the monitor soon confirm what we already know: my mother-in-law is indeed leaving us. I lean across the crisp white bed sheet and whisper to her, "Please get in touch with us. Let us know that you're OK."

Awkwardness fills the air as the body language of others registers varying levels of discomfort with and disapproval of my request.

Shortly thereafter, her struggle ends as the dreaded flat line takes away any hope. Her last breath is drawn, her pulse soon stops. My mother-in-law has physically taken leave of the people she loved most in this world.

We stare in disbelief at the physical shell. *Is it really possible that she is gone? Where did she go? How did this happen?* The grief feels insurmountable; it is our first death-bed experience.

As we leave the emergency room, Peter chides me: "Don't you think that was a lot of responsibility to place on my poor dying mother?" Although said in jest, I know he had not been comfortable with my request.

From there, I go directly to my own mother's bedside but choose not to tell her of my mother-in-law's passing for fear of upsetting her. They were close once – both named Amelia – but due to their respective conditions had not seen each other in years.

I feel so heartsick over the unexpected scene just witnessed and wish I could talk about it with my own mother. After all, we were all geared up to lose her first.

The Visitor

The next day I am amazed at how unusually alert and lucid my mother is. We chat for a while, and I feed her. She then casually says, "I wonder if my visitor will come again today."

She has many visitors from Hospice, and I wonder who in particular she is looking forward to seeing. "Which visitor, Mom?" I ask.

"Peter's mother," she says.

I try to sound light: "Peter's mother was here?"

"Yes."

"When?"

"Yesterday afternoon."

The day of her passing, I realize. I try not to sound overanxious, but my heart is pounding wildly.

"What did she say?"

"She said not to neglect Peter's father during this time. I told her we wouldn't ever ignore anyone!"

My mother then moves on to other topics, unaware of the significance of the message. Again, I choose not to tell her of my mother-in-law's passing. But I know my mother-in-law has indeed paid her a visit, has fulfilled my request through the woman I love most in this world. It also gives me such incredible relief to know that my mother-in-law, a kind and gentle woman, will be there when it is my mother's turn to cross over.

I fully intend to make the same request of my mother, and this time my husband will understand.

My Mother Died

I am embarrassed to admit that I had been jealous of Peter having two "healthy" parents – and somewhat angry that one of mine would likely be the first to go. But then fate threw us a curve when Peter's mother died unexpectedly.

"My mother died," I heard Peter tell someone on the phone.

Those words seem unspeakable, incomprehensible. How is he even able to string them together coherently? How can he carry on his own life after qualifying to say those words? You must forever mark in your brain the date and hour when you lose your mother.

"The world moves on," laments Peter's father after the passing of his wife of 68 years. But how can it when your loved one has died?

I watch the scene unfold like some macabre dress rehearsal as to what awaits with my own mother. And in some bizarre way, I am now jealous that Peter is experiencing the death of a parent first, with all the outpouring of sympathy and support. And that for him (and his mother), it is already over.

How screwed up is that?

Flashbacks

I embarked on this journey with a "no regrets" policy. I pledged to do whatever it took so that when it was all over, I would have no regrets. I am not one who can live with regret.

Every decision I made, I tried to make in my mother's best interest. She came first, before my job, my husband, my friends, my father – and especially myself. I should be able to sleep with a clear conscience when she passes on. Except for...the demons of the past.

Flashbacks mercilessly haunt me. *But I didn't know*, I tell myself. *I didn't know.* Then I wonder if that's true – did I really not know she was ailing, or did I dismiss it for its inconvenience? I knew she was unsteady on her feet – even saw her fall several times. I knew she was spilling things – saw that too. I knew she went to the grocery store and the bank and stood in their doorways until someone asked if they could help, because she was too tired to walk any further.

"I have no energy," she told me on the phone.

"You're just depressed," I lamely offered. After all, there was plenty to be depressed about.

When the Florida nursing home social worker told me my mother couldn't live alone much longer, I responded that she didn't know my mother! My mother was just overwhelmed with caring for my father! Yet I knew my mother was scared and cried a lot. I knew she asked me to stay with her in Florida longer than I had planned each visit.

But I also knew she told me not to worry, that nothing would happen to her. She told me most convincingly that she did not have a brain tumor. She told me she was OK. And I believed her, this strong, invincible woman.

And then the call after her emergency room visit, advising me of a numb left arm. And still, she was left alone in Florida for months with only weekend visits until found on the bathroom floor by her friends, unable to get up, having clawed at the door, too proud to use her medic alert alarm.

Yes, I experience many flashbacks from that time before the diagnosis. But I don't seem to have any regrets since, at least not yet. Except perhaps regrets for my own diminishing stamina and diminishing relationships. And for my lack of knowing that I knew sooner...

> *Crippling flashbacks continued several months after her death. It was so hard to forget the experience of watching my mother die.*

A Tender Farewell

"She's not well, Dad," I tell him when I pick him up to go visit his wife.

"Is she alive?" he asks.

"Yes, but she's very sick."

"Then let's go now."

He is quieter than usual on the ride there. Even Dean Martin's *Volare* doesn't interest him. He is tense being wheeled through the halls of her "place." I put a party hat on him to lighten the mood.

And then we see her – all dressed up sitting in a chair. I wheel him up to her right side and say, "Daddy's here, Mom."

"I know. How could I miss him?" she responds with a faint smile. His relief is apparent.

"You scared me!" he loudly accuses.

"I'm sorry, Dad. I was scared too."

"I know," he says.

He eats the lunch I brought for him; I attempt to feed my mother without much luck. He observes, cheering on every mouthful.

"I don't feel well," he says a short time later, his nerves no doubt frayed.

She begins to doze. "Say goodbye to Daddy," I tell her.

She opens her eyes and says, "Goodbye, dear." She gently touches the contours of his face as he kisses her hand.

"I'll be back next week," he tells her. "Will you still be here?"

"Next week?" she asks, looking pensive. But she does not answer the question. I extricate his arm from her grip, and we head to the elevators. "She didn't want me to leave," he says.

"Do you want to go back?" I ask.

"Yes, can we?"

We head back to the room, where she has been put in bed. She is no longer lucid and does not respond. He holds her hand for a few more minutes, and soon we leave for the second time.

"Poor kid," he says of his 88-year-old wife. "Poor kid. Is her cough dangerous?"

"I don't know," I lie.

"Will she be OK?"

"I don't know," I lie again.

> *This visit marked the last time my parents were able to speak to each other.*

Last Rites and Human Rights

The priest comes to anoint her and to give her "the sacrament of the sick." She cries her silent cry.

"Why are you crying, Amelia?" Father Keating asks.

She hesitates. And I'm wondering why he is asking such a stupid question at a time like this. *She's crying because she's dying!!*

She then shocks us both by responding, "I'm crying because my church won't allow women to become priests."

He is unnerved: "You're crying about that *now*?"

"Yes," she defiantly answers.

"Why?"

"Because if I had wanted to become a priest, the church

wouldn't have let me."

"Did you want to be a priest, Amelia?"

"No, but I would have wanted to have that choice."

I grin from ear to ear at her spunk despite the gravity of the situation. On his way out, the retired priest tells me he has NEVER had anyone challenge the dogma of the Catholic Church on her deathbed. That's my mom! What a privilege it is to be privy to her attempt to slay one more dragon standing in the way of human rights.

Later, I ask her what intercessions she would choose if she were planning a mass, in hopes of being able to use them at her funeral.

She looks thoughtful and then says, "I can't."

"You can't what?"

"I can't use the ones I'd want because the priest would be mad at me."

That clearly never stopped her before.

Nothing Left

It was finally time to take down the Never Give Up *poster we had hung in her room.*

There is nothing left to say.
Nothing left to do.
Nothing left to fix.
There is nothing left of her.
Except...the end.

Save her!
Fix her!

Do something!

I can't believe this is happening.
Not to my mother.
It's all so surreal.
I watch it but don't believe it.
It's so hard to just let someone go.

Our culture tells us to preserve life at all cost.
We struggled so long and hard to keep her alive.
It seems unnatural to give up now.
But it is time.
There is nothing left to do.

Last Words

"You're going to be an angel, Mama," I tell her.
"You're my angel," she responds.
"And when you are, please come visit me."
"I will. I love you, dolly," she says as the last coherent statement of her life.

Poor Girl

She is so sick that he does not recognize her. My sister and I wheel him up to her bedside and still he does not realize that this is his wife.

"Who is this?" he asks. "Where's the other one?"

My sister and I inappropriately start laughing, out of sheer exhaustion. We quickly gain control and convince Dad that this shell is his wife. He becomes sorrowful and tender. He holds her hand, kisses her, shouts "I love you" in her ear, and tries to feed her. He tenderly touches her face and neck, telling her that she's beautiful.

"How are you feeling, dear? OK?" He is so used to her being so strong and expects her bravado to re-emerge. She is comatose.

It is their 63rd wedding anniversary.

We sit for a while until he reluctantly agrees to leave, only after being promised he can soon return. She shows no acknowledgement, save for the tear in the corner of her eye, which he dabs with a tissue.

Later that night, I stop to see him and find him crying in bed. Without prompting, he explains, "I didn't know it was her. I couldn't believe it." I tell him I understand.

"I love her," he says. "I really love that girl."

I start to tell him more specifics about her medical status, but he stops me. "Don't," he says and keeps repeating, "Poor girl. Poor girl." He knows his 88-year-old "girl" is leaving him, but he doesn't want to know the gory details.

"We'll get through this, Dad," I tell him. "We'll be sad together, but we'll get through it."

"OK," he says. "I'm glad you came to see me tonight."

Little did he know, I was the one who needed him.

Wonderful and Amazing

I lie in bed with her – a full body hug. She is still, with no recognition of my presence. I speak to her softly through my tears: "You are so wonderful and amazing, Mama. I hope I am worthy to be your daughter. Everyone says I am like you; I hope I am."

She remains stiff and silent. Suddenly Robert, a nurse's aide, enters the room. He drops to his knees next to the bed and says to me, out of the blue, "You are wonderful and amazing. I just felt I had to tell you that."

He leaves as quickly as he enters. I am dumbstruck.

Days later, I ask Robert why he did that. He tells me he doesn't know; he just felt drawn to the room and compelled to tell me that even though he is not assigned to my mother's care.

"I can't explain it," he says, as puzzled as I and a little embarrassed. "I just had to do it."

I thank my mother for answering me, even though she herself can no longer speak.

Unconvincing

"I'm OK, Mama.

Go.

Go to the light.

It's a beautiful place.

God is waiting for you.

Everyone you've been praying for all these years is waiting to
     thank you.

You'll be an angel, Mama.

You'll soar above us all.

It's OK, Mama.

You can go.
I would go with you if I could.
But I know you wouldn't want that.

All your business is in order.
Everything is all set, just like you wanted it.
You can leave, Mama.
I'm OK.
Don't let the tears running down my cheeks hold you back."

Confusion

"Are you mad at me, Mama? Did I do something wrong?"

I desperately peer into her face, exhausted, confused and delusional over her silence, the physical changes, her vacant eyes.

I want to catch a glimpse of my "real" mother ("the other one"), the mother who cast nothing but love and approval my way. This expressionless face I now see frightens me, confuses me. I interpret her lack of expression as anger.

Although she is comatose, I fear she may rise up and yell at me or strike me, something she has never done. I sense her inner frustration and rage. She is furious that this has happened to her, yet she never acted that out – she was too genteel. But I sense it now – she is still in the anger stage of loss. No wonder she is not ready to pass over. She has not arrived at acceptance yet.

She has suffered so many indignities for such a dignified woman. Yet her proud countenance is holding up until the end.

"Are you mad at me, Mama," I again ask and immediately regret that I am foolish enough to even utter those words. *Forgive me, Mama.*

If I Had It to Do Over

"Life can only be understood backward, yet must be lived forward."
           - Kierkegaard

We didn't know how it would turn out. But then again, we never do. We never know when we set a course if we're doing the right thing. We only know when it's too late.

If I had it to do over, I wouldn't have put my mother through the radiation treatments. I wouldn't have kept her in the hospital for ten weeks. I would have brought her home and helped her live out the rest of her life without extreme medical intervention. I would have just enjoyed what time we had left instead of having her suffer the trauma of radiation to her brain – emotional and physical trauma. Because quality of life is more important than quantity.

I know this now; I didn't know it before we went through it. Because at such a desperate time, it seemed like our only hope, our only option to save her. How could we refuse a treatment that might work? We wanted to throw everything we had at this so that there would be no regrets.

But now…there are different regrets. Regrets that we did choose radiation and hospitalization. Yet…if it had worked…

Life is full of regrets for things done and not done, said and not said. There are no guarantees, and all we can do is trust our instincts and make the best decisions we can at the time. Then brace ourselves for the regret that will inevitably follow.

A Regret Unfounded

The Hospice nurse arrives at my mother's room to find me distraught. Despite the obvious, she asks why I am so upset.

"I regret putting her through those ten weeks of radiation," I tell Jane. "It didn't help one bit, and it kept her institutionalized for so long. I think it did more harm than good."

"I strongly disagree," she says. She goes on to tell me about typical brain tumor patients and the intolerable pain they feel: they scream, they rock, they vomit from the pain of cranial pressure.

"Your mother is peaceful in her condition. The radiation shrunk the tumor enough to relieve the pressure, and that was an excellent thing you did for your mother. Her end of life experience is better because of the radiation. And because of the reiki you performed."

I later tell Gayle of the conversation, and she confirms what Jane told me: "My friend's mother had a brain tumor, and she said you don't know pain and suffering unless you've been through that. Did your mother have terrible headaches? Did she scream at you in anger because of her pain?"

My answer to both of these questions is no. Perhaps the radiation helped after all. No regrets...no regrets.

After she died, I told the radiologist that if I had known she would have only lived five months after her treatment, I wouldn't have put her through it. He said the radiation's purpose was to improve the quality of her remaining time, not to extend it. I'm not sure we fully understood that going in.

Real People

There are no monitors. No beeping gadgets to tell us that life is leaving. Just real people taking her pulse, listening to her heart, looking at her. Real people looking at a real person dying and assessing what is in her best interest.

They describe the indicators that death is near, what they're looking for when they examine her. I don't know whether to hope the indicators are there or not. I passively watch them, scared to hear their report.

The oxygen machine makes a loud hum in the room, reminding us that her condition is worsening. But I don't need a machine to tell me she is leaving. I feel it deep in my soul.

Every Breath You Take

> "Her heart is so strong," the nurse said. "She's not going to give up easily." And she didn't.

I watch her closely. Each breath. And as I watch, I hope this won't be her last.

And I hope it will.

Her chest moves up and down imperceptibly. The movement is much less dramatic now, the breathing shallow.

With each breath, my mother is still alive. With each breath, my mother is still suffering. So may this breath be her last…or not.

Die.

Don't die!

Die.

Don't die!

Take a breath!

Stop breathing.

Take a breath!

Stop breathing.

No wonder she lingers. My message is mixed and confusing, although unspoken.

The Prayers, They Come Back

I wonder what I could do to help her pass. It seems I have said and done everything imaginable...except pray over her.

I start with a *Hail Mary,* then the *Our Father.* Although not verbalized for years, The Rosary takes shape in my mouth. I say those Catholic prayers that were her lifeblood, although they seem foreign to me.

She always wanted me to say The Rosary – "It's a form of meditation," she'd tell me, trying to appeal to my more spiritual side. But I never could (or would) do it with her. Yet in her honor, I can somehow do it now – for her, if not with her.

In a desperate moment, I return to my roots – the words sound hauntingly familiar and right for the time. What if she has been holding out all this time for me to finally say The Rosary?

> *Hail Mary, full of grace,*
> *The Lord is with thee.*
> *Blessed art thou amongst women,*
> *And blessed is the fruit of thy womb, Jesus.*
> *Holy Mary, Mother of God,*
> *Pray for us sinners,*
> *Now and at the hour of our death. Amen.*

Perhaps the real miracle here is that at some point or another during her illness, my mother got her lapsed Catholic husband and two daughters to say The Rosary. A lifelong ambition fulfilled at the hour of her death. *Amen.*

Goodnight, Mama

> *I lay next to her in the cot for a week. She had become*
> *my whole life; I could not leave her as she took leave of*

her own.

January 29
"Goodnight, Mama."
I don't know if we'll both be here tomorrow.

January 30
"Goodnight, Mama."
Is this our last night together? I hope not...I hope so.

January 31
Last night was our last night together, Mama.
I am stricken with grief...I am relieved.

Goodbye, Mama

> *"What will you do when she dies?" my sister asked over*
> *the phone. "I don't know," I responded. "What are my*
> *choices?"*

My mother died today at 6:57a.m.

After months of pain and suffering, she looks so beautiful to me when her struggle finally ends.

I kiss and hug her one last time.

I stroke her cheek.

I fix her hair.

I hold her hand.

I say goodbye to my mother.

But I do not let go until they wheel her away.

Aftershock

> *"I still remember how terrible it feels to lose your*
> *mother. I still want to call my mother to tell her*
> *something that happened to me."*
> *-Martha, 85 years old*

Words do not easily come to such an empty soul.
I ache for my loss.
My soulmate is gone.
And I will miss her every day for the rest of my life.

I am powered by adrenaline, running on empty.
The hole in my heart is there, but I plod along, behaving as if
    I can handle it.
I can't.
I am so empty.

A great vacuum exists, sucking the air out of me.
Yet, strangely, I feel strong at the same time.
Strong in my knowledge that I did everything I could to
    save her.
And strong in my conviction to carry on in her name.

Breaking the News

I don't want to tell him right away; I even hope somehow he'll already know. Perhaps she would visit him, as she was visited by my mother-in-law.

I go to his bedside and tell my father that I have some bad news for him.

"No, no, no," he begs, as if he could make it not true.

"Mom didn't wake up this morning," I continue.

He drops his head into his hands and sobs. To try to distract him, I take him out for breakfast, but he is unable to eat or drink anything. Understandably so. Everything sticks in my throat as well.

I do more than break the news; I break his heart.

I want to help him through it, but I need help myself.

Part Ten: The Abyss

The Abyss

I wake up and my mother is still dead.

I Was There

You took your last breath.
I was there, in the cot next to you.
But was I asleep or awake?
I remember waking and seeing you breathing.
I drifted back to sleep, thinking we had more time.
Yet when I awakened again, time was up.
I thought I saw you take your last few breaths.
But now, I fear it was already over.
And I was just witnessing your body's release.
I hope you know I was there.
I wish I had held you longer.
I wish I had never let you go.
But I was there, Mama. I was there.

Nothing

There is nothing I want to do.
Nothing.
Even lying in bed is unsatisfactory.
It takes a heroic effort to pick up this pen.
Depression.
Exhaustion.
Fear.
Anger.
Nothingness.

I Didn't Know

I didn't know my mother had been suffering from headaches for over a year. She never mentioned them to me.

I didn't know an audiologist had told her years ago that he saw something in her ear that might be a tumor. She never mentioned it to me.

I didn't know that no one survives a malignant brain tumor – that it was a death sentence from Day One. No one mentioned it to me.

I didn't know that my mother was the lead in her high school play called "Stray Cats."

I didn't know I had so many good friends.

I didn't know that my relationship with my sister was beyond redemption.

I learn all this at my mother's funeral.

The Rose

It looks so lovely as you walk toward it at the nurses' station. It brightens the sterile environment, adding color and grace. And then you remember the rose is a tribute, in memory of someone who has recently died. Its appearance symbolizes loss.

An aide writes to tell me that the rose last week bore my mother's name: "I am learning to detest those roses. I understand why they're there and can appreciate the sentiment. But what they are coming to represent to me is an empty place. One less greeting to start my day, one less goodnight to end it."

Although I am not there to see it, for me that rose represents the greatest loss I will ever sustain. How can such a delicate flower bear up under the pressure?

I am Functioning

I have suffered the greatest loss of my life.

Yet, I am functioning.

I can talk about other things.

I can socialize.

I can work.

I can even laugh.

I can act as if everything is OK.

Yet, it is only an act – trying to convince myself that I can survive this.

Everything seems as if in slow motion.

I move through gelatinous air.

My balance – physical and emotional – is off.

I am so tired.

But I am no longer worried.

When the worst possible thing has happened, what is left to
    worry about?

While it is sad to not have reason to worry anymore – to not
    be *able* to worry any more,

The sense of responsibility is gone.

So I am lighter.

And, oh, so much sadder.

Yet, I am functioning.

The Secret Society

We don't have a secret handshake, but we could. We don't have
a clubhouse or membership dues, officers or bylaws. Yet we are a
billion-member secret society with a very steep price for admittance: losing a parent.

In talking to other 50-something year olds, few have not been
initiated into this club. But they can only fully talk about it with
other members. Because there is no way for non-members to understand the depth of the discussion. Sure, they empathize and
say socially appropriate things. But they don't fully get it.

It's not their fault. There is no way to know how it feels unless
you have gone through it. They don't yet know the intensity of
the pain of having their hearts ripped out.

Words cannot adequately convey the experience of what it
feels like to lose a parent. You can't even begin to imagine it; you
just have to wait until you are inducted. And then long for the
days when you were blissfully unaware that the exclusive club
even existed.

Is That You, Mama?

*I picked up the little brittle case on which my mother
had long ago drawn a map of all the places they lived
while my dad was in the Army Air Corps. I've had it for
over 20 years, yet never opened it. Tonight I did. "We'll
meet again," it said inside, in my mother's handwriting.
I sent it to my sister.*

I feel something on the bed. Like the dog. But more like someone sitting on the edge of the bed. In my dream-like state, I push
it with my foot, and it disappears. And I wonder, *Is that you,
Mama?*

I am so eager for and open to contact from her. Yet I don't
know if it's happening. I thought it would be obvious, thought I
would know without question. But I don't recognize her; I don't
know of her presence.

I look for her; I wait for her. I expect her at any moment.

I check out every subtlety and wonder, *Is that you, Mama? Are
you here with me? Are you the reason Dad was in such a good
mood yesterday?*

*You promised you'd be back, Mama. You always said that, for
years now. And I didn't doubt it for a second. Until now. Until the
silence.*

*Others tell me you'll be back – I just have to be patient. We're not
very good at that, Mama. I am frustrated by my inability to make it
happen. Perhaps you are too.*

*I don't know what to look for. But I look for you...everywhere,
every day.*

Is that you, Mama?

Depressed

I awake depressed.

There is nothing I want to do.

Except talk to her – the only one who can make me feel better.

Yet her death is the reason I am depressed.

Who can make me feel better now?

Friends tell me she gave me the skills to make myself feel better.

I'm not so sure…I depended on her for that.

Mom, It's My Birthday II

Sympathy cards intermingled with birthday cards, left unopened for weeks. I don't want to be the recipient of sympathy cards, don't like that honor bestowed. I am overwhelmed by the kindness but paralyzed by the reality of what they represent.

It's my birthday, Mom – the day you birthed me, the day our lives were forevermore entwined. Thank you for bringing me to life.

I miss hearing your voice on the phone saying, "Happy birthday, dolly." But I hear it in my head and treasure it ever more.

Kathy didn't call me, but I didn't expect her to. I called Dad to hear his greeting when prompted. But I feel alone, Mama. And oh, how I miss you.

Mine is the first birthday you are not here for…and it is the first of my birthdays that I won't have you. Perhaps it gets easier – but I don't want to be immune from the pain of losing you. It stands as a hallmark of my deep abiding affection.

I love you, Mama. Thanks for this day.

Moving On

> *"The worst part of losing one of my 'friends' here is*
> *walking in and seeing an empty bed," an aide told me.*
> *"It helps when someone else fills the bed because then*
> *you have another soul to care for."*

They were disappointed when told the funeral service would be out of town. "We need a chance to grieve too. Will there be a local memorial service?" her caregivers asked.

For them, I schedule a local service three weeks after the burial in Rochester. As the day approaches, I become anxious. What if no one comes? I don't want my mother (or myself) to be embarrassed by low turnout. I call Hospice and the nursing home to remind staff. One by one, they beg off, with valid excuses.

Although the church is filled with my friends, only three of her caregivers are in attendance.

They have necessarily moved on. The bed has been filled; there is another new soul to care for. If they grieve substantially for everyone they lose, they will be depleted of energy to give the next. I understand.

I like to think my mother was special to them, and she was… while she was still here.

> *The local service gave my father a chance to attend*
> *his wife's memorial. We did not take him to the*
> *funeral four hours away based on his nursing home's*
> *recommendation. At the service, he kept looking around*
> *for the casket, loudly repeating, "Where is she?"*

Eulogy for His Wife

The day after the memorial service, I stop to see how my dad is doing. He is happy to see me and immediately says, "I wish I had said something yesterday."

"What would you have said?" I ask.

"I would have said she worked a lot and was never home."

I don't know whether to laugh or cry. It's more true than not, but I am amazed that he can remember and articulate it. He asks me again where she is, and I tell him she's buried in a cemetery. He responds, "Oh, is she?" seemingly happy that she's been put to rest. I tell him yes, and that he will someday be with her again. He seems content with that notion.

Her Boots

I went looking for them.
The suede tan boots of hers.
I don't know why I saved them.
They are stylish but well worn.
I put them on with my jeans.
And just walk around my house.
They don't fit quite right.
But they are the boots that held my mother's feet.
They traveled part of her journey with her.
And that's good enough for me.

I'll Never Know

I'll never know now who left that needle in the framed needle-point.

I'll never know which orange glassware was the wedding gift from her mother. Or which broach belonged to Mrs. McKennon.

Or where she got the little turquoise dish.

It seemed there'd always be an opportunity to ask – we'd get to it someday. By the time I realized I was losing my chance, she no longer remembered. And now that she is dead, there is no one I can ask.

I'll never know. That window has slammed shut.

Available

When we arrive at the Mardi Gras party, my father is given beads and a mask and proceeds to dance in his wheelchair. The aides dance with him and then...they match him up with other women. He holds their hands.

I watch as he dances with a sweet elderly woman, and tears fill my eyes. I sadly realize he is now "available." I wonder if the aides consciously recognize the change in his status when they match him up. And I wonder if he knows it. He seems more interested in the women than I had noticed before but wonder if it's just me. I only know I don't like it.

His availability only means my mother is gone. And while I don't want him to be sad or lonely, I do want him to have a respectable mourning period – whatever that means. And to realize that she cannot be replaced.

Freaked

> "You know how you always know your mother's there, even when you're not with her?" said Peggy Jo. "Well, that's the way it is when she's gone too – you'll always know she's gone."

When I allow myself to know that my mother is dead, I begin to freak out. When I allow the realization into my consciousness,

I am overwhelmed with panic and despair. How can I go on without her?

If I go my merry way and bury the naked truth deep inside of me – so deep that it doesn't register – I can limp along. But when I know – really KNOW she is dead – I find myself whimpering with an infantile helplessness, until I can forget once more.

Kryptonite

I have lost my power. I have lost my ability to control outcomes. Worse yet, I no longer believe that I should even try. My influence has shrunk – my fighting spirit beaten down.

Kryptonite has rendered me impotent.

Kryptonite has stripped me of all illusions.

Kryptonite is reality.

Daughters United

"When I see someone smiling or having fun, I want to ask them, 'Is your mother still alive?'" says Mary Anne. Because it seems to her that person could not be so carefree if her mother were dead.

As my flashbacks of my mother's final days become more intense, Hospice recommends a Daughters' Bereavement Group to help me articulate the depth of loss I feel. I join ten other women who are now orphaned by one or both parents. I wish my sister were among them, but we are grieving separately, in our own ways.

The women and I tell our stories, each depicting our mothers as being more saintly than the next – except for deserting us. Our devastation is mirrored back to each of us by the other women who sit in this weekly circle. I no longer feel alone in my grief.

They tell me that the second year of the loss is greater. First time through, the experience is unique and seems temporary. Then the second birthday or Christmas, it becomes real. It's permanent; she's not coming back.

"The only thing worse than losing a parent is losing a child," the facilitator says, validating the deep pain we are all in. *Why didn't anyone ever warn me it would be this hard?* Yet, it is likely that I would not have understood anyway.

Those who have lost both parents tell me how precious the last parent becomes after losing the first. They talk of the compounded loss and devastation when both are gone. There is no one left to tell them stories of their past, no one who knows them so thoroughly. Surprisingly, siblings often become alienated from each other as well.

I'm glad I stopped to see my father before I went to the meeting. And so very glad that I still have him. I will try to do the very best I can for him despite my darkest hour.

I'm OK Until…

…my dad asks for her.

…I see Sue's mom visiting for the weekend.

…I see someone shopping with her mother.

…I have flashbacks of her illness.

…I realize the worst that could happen did.

…I start to buy or prepare food for her.

…I want to know what she's thinking about current events.

…I remember she's gone.

Gardenias

Joyce calls to see how I am doing. I tell her I know my mother is "in a better place," but I still have sad moments because I miss her so much.

Joyce suggests I ask my mother to give me a sign of the joy she is experiencing in her new dimension: "For instance, ask her to show you her favorite flower as a symbol of her new-found joy."

When I tell Joyce that gardenias were her favorite, she laughs and says, "Well, that's not a flower you typically see – not like roses or daisies. Good luck with that one! Pick something else."

We both laugh and go on to other topics.

Three days later, I pay my first return visit to the nursing home where my mother died. With a lump in my throat, I go in. Memories come flooding in as I wait for the elevator; I want to turn and run.

The door opens and there, in the elevator display case, are two silk gardenias! Plain as day! *No,* I say to myself. *This can't be. You're inventing this.*

I closely scrutinize the flowers. *They're roses,* I determine. But upon closer inspection, there is no denying the large silky cream-colored petals are definitely NOT roses; they are gardenias.

My heart leaps with joy and gratitude for having been shown a symbol of my mother's new-found joy, as Joyce had framed it for me.

I spot 90-year-old Emily in her wheelchair in the hallway. I tell her I have heard from my mother. Without hesitation, she tells me that she had heard from her daughter after she passed as well.

"After that, I didn't cry anymore," Emily tells me.

Answered Desperation

In all the piles of paper, so disorganized and scattered, I immediately found the information I need to help settle the estate. I didn't even know what I was looking for, what the attorney wanted. But you did, didn't you, Mom? And you led me right to it.

You are making yourself known to me. Stay near me, Mom. I feel so overwhelmed and still need you. And...thank you for your help tonight.

Part Eleven: I Wish It Were Like Before

I Wish It Were Like Before

I pick him up at the appointed hour on Saturday morning. He gets all bundled up to brave the winter chill, and we head to the car. But this morning, our destination is different. Instead of going to see my mother, we are running errands and going out to lunch.

We listen to a Dean Martin CD and make small talk. Although I am painfully aware of the itinerary change, he seems perfectly content to sit in the car as I race in and out of stores.

I then glance over at him as I'm driving and notice his eyes welled up with tears. I ask him what's wrong, and he responds, "I wish it were like before, when we used to go see your mother."

I stroke his head and express shared sadness. I am surprised that he feels that void and am grateful to have someone to grieve with.

I wish it were like before too, Dad. Way before – before you broke your hip, before Mom got sick. And I realize that someday this moment might be the "before" I am wishing for.

Wistful

Why would we not be wistful?
Time moves us along.
From one passage to another.
We can only look back.
We can never go back.

It happens before we know it.
We enter the next stage of life.
Not realizing that life is not really a continuum.
But rather a set of discrete blocks of time.
We leave one behind as we enter the next.

Why would we not be wistful?

A Terrible Mistake

She can't be dead. It's not possible. I keep expecting her to show up, to put an end to all this nonsense about her being dead.

I keep thinking we'll have another chance, that it'll be like before. That I should save those clothes because she'll need them when she returns.

It's all just a terrible mistake. *Come back, Mama. We'll get everything all straightened out.*

She can't be dead. NOOOOOOOOOOOOOO!!!!!!!!!!

New Shoes

I threw your shoes out today, Mama. The little brown suede ones. They looked practically brand new, like you never wore them. Were you saving them for "good?"

I carried them around with me for weeks because I didn't know what to do with them. I kept them in the back seat of my car until – until I had to once more face that you are really gone.

I'm sorry I put them in the garbage can. But you won't need those shoes, Mama. In fact, you haven't for a year. Yet even today, I still thought maybe I should save them for you.

If you come back, I'll buy you a new pair. Deal?

> *I continued to speak to her often, as if she could hear, as if she were here.*

Last Dance

Club Maplewood, they called it. A dance at the nursing home, complete with disco lights, a Tom Jones-type performer, ginger-ale champagne, and a wide-open dance floor. A dance floor lined with 70 walkers and wheelchairs.

As part of the entertainment, there are expert ballroom dancers performing choreographed routines. They twirl each other around the dance floor as the wheelchair-bound residents sit, solemn-faced, on the sidelines and watch. My discomfort is palpable. *How cruel to subject the residents to this spectacle! Do the fancy dancers realize that although they might be superior in their abilities now, the same fate might befall them someday?* I am convinced that this so-called "dance" is a bad idea. A really bad idea. I want to leave and take my dad with me.

Then the magic begins to unfold, like a scene from the movie *Cocoon*. People start to tap their feet and clap their hands. The performer sings to the elderly women, and they swoon. And slowly, other dancers join the pros on the dance floor. The aides work the room, holding up those with walkers who move slowly but in time to the rhythm. Wheelchairs begin to appear, and residents are twirled by partners with two good legs.

I realize at this moment that there is a dancer in every one of us, no matter our age, and even when the flesh gets weak, the spirit remains willing.

The scene is not lost on my father. He comments on how good the dancers are, looking at me intently. "Do you want to dance?" I ask him hesitantly. "No," he says, giving me a moment of relief before adding, "Unless you want to?"

With much reservation, I wheel my dad onto the now-crowded dance floor. We start to dance, this little man "standing" three feet high in his wheelchair and me in my high heels and business suit. We dance the jitterbug, holding both hands and moving back and forth. Despite his diminished stature, he insists on leading and on twirling me, for which I have to stoop considerably. He grins.

Cameras flash. The scene is nothing less than extraordinary. We dance for the rest of the evening until the last song: *Last Dance*. And there, at the nursing home disco, I dance what is likely to be my last dance with my father. His eyes sparkle; mine fill with tears.

While I am tired, my father could have kept going, way past his bedtime. We are among the last to leave the event. And as

I wheel him down the hall, two of the professional dancers approach him.

"You were good," he tells them.

"No, you were good!" they respond almost simultaneously. They introduce themselves to him and ask for his name. They tell him they loved watching him dance, that he has great rhythm and so much enthusiasm. They tell him it was a privilege to be on the same dance floor with him.

He could have burst with pride, thanks to their kindness and sensitivity. And I am delighted to have my skepticism proven unwarranted for the second time that evening.

I take him to his little room, and we say goodnight. "Thank you for dancing with me, Dad," I say, as I turn to go.

"Did you have fun?" he asks.

"Yes," I respond emphatically. For it was truly the best dance I have ever attended.

Moments

> *"We can't back up," Peggy Jo reminded me. "We can't back up."*

Surely we must be able to reclaim those past moments in time. Those moments we thought would last forever but, in truth, were only a blink of an eye.

Why can't I be young and carefree again?

Why doesn't my mother come back?

Why can't I take my dad back home to see his friends?

Where did those opportunities go? How can it all be so fleeting? We must be able to reclaim those experiences – we just have to rewind and get them back, right? They're not gone forever...

are they?

And by mourning those moments that defy reclamation now, am I missing the present moments, which I will someday long for?

The Emergency Room

The chest pain is so great that they send him to the hospital. We ride in the ambulance together on this Friday night and wait six hours for a diagnosis: pneumonia and a urinary tract infection.

As we lie on the stretcher together awaiting the next test, I hug the disoriented, trembling man. And I send out this message to my mother:

I'm doing the best I can to take care of Dad in your absence. I hope I'm doing it well enough for you. I don't want to lose him yet, but if you want him to be with you, I understand. I can't be selfish, Mom, because I know how much you loved him. He'd rather be with you anyway.

I will not compete with my mother for him. My parents really should be together – for reasons I can't fully comprehend but now know to be true. But while he is still mine to care for, I will do the very best I can – for all of us.

Role Reversal

They send him "home" the next day, and he feels slightly better. But I sense it's temporary.

"I was worried about you," he tells me.

"Why?" I ask.

"Because you were sick, and we had to go to the hospital."

Perhaps my father and I have become one too, in his eyes.

Or perhaps this role reversal is hard for him to comprehend – fathers are supposed to take care of their daughters, not the other way around.

The Privilege

I have the privilege of holding my almost 90-year-old father's hand. I have the privilege of stroking his white hair and putting cream on his dry face. I have the privilege of seeing his face light up when I arrive and crestfallen when I leave. I have the privilege of knowing he loves me, and I love him. The past is the past; we have transcended that struggle.

I have the privilege of him calling me by my mother's name. "You were a good golfer," he tells her via my personage. And I now carry the burden that she carried of taking care of him. I share her joy and sorrow at the opportunity lost and gained.

Do I do this for her or for him…or for myself?

What Happened, Dad?

We watched Jack Nicklaus play his last golf tournament on TV. "He's old," my father said of the man 25 years his junior.

As we watch the Mets game, he says, "I wish I could just go back there and play."

I size him up in his wheelchair. "Could you run fast?" I ask him.

"Why sure!"

"What position did you used to play?"

"First base," he proudly answers.

"That's an important position."

"Of course! What did you think?" he indignantly replies.

What happened, Dad? I silently wonder. *What happened to your body? How did it get so weak and frail? Did you ever once think your virile body would betray you like this? Are you aware that you have changed, that you are an old man? Why this cruel fate?*

What happened, Dad?

Photographs and Memories

Photos only serve to remind me that that moment has passed, that we can never return to that time and that I wish I had been more present when I had the opportunity to experience that moment immortalized on film.

For what is the benefit of remembering that someone was once young if now all you see is a time-ravaged body? It seems cruel to keep a pictorial documentary of the decline in appearance and ability.

We act like it won't happen to us. Our coping mechanisms register such compensatory beliefs so as to suggest that some people are born old – this isn't a trajectory we are all on. Perhaps that is the reason for the photographs – to remind us that the clock ticks and the bell tolls for all.

Fleeting

I can't not know that they're fleeting.
Youth.
Beauty.
Ability.

I face it every day, sense it every action.
Someday soon, I won't be able to do, know, remember.

Mirrors and my hands will betray me.
Just like what they experienced.

Fleeting.
How much better to not be aware of this,
Every waking, breathing minute of my life.
But I can't return there.

I am here now.
After watching all their despair and suffering.
My parents didn't think it would end like this.
But now I know it does.

And I can't forget that it does.
Try as I might to block it out.
I live in that consciousness.
Ever aware that what we hold so dear is fleeting.

Worried Friends

I open yet another piece of mail forwarded to my mother:
> *There has been no reply from you in so long – have
> tried to find out how you are both doing?!!! We have
> been friends for so many years – I'm heartbroken that I
> haven't heard from you. Would one of your daughters
> be so kind to let me know in case you can't? Would
> really appreciate it. I'm praying for you both.*

There must be many friends out there who are wondering why
they didn't get a Christmas card or a call last year. I decide to call
Charlotte in Illinois, a woman I've always heard about but never
met.

I hear the anxiety in her voice as I identify myself. "My mother died January 31st," I tell her as I unexpectedly sob into the phone. She begins to cry too. "Oh, I knew something had to be terribly wrong. We always stayed in touch."

I update her on my dad's situation. She tells me they were Army Air Corps buddies, friends for over sixty years. She tells me she and Vince now live in assisted living, where there are more wheelchairs every day.

I tell Charlotte that a picture of Vince and her was in my mother's purse when my mother went into the hospital and was still in there when I brought the purse home without her.

Those were the days, my friend. They thought they'd never end.

Dad's Back

> *One pill made him more responsive but mean; one pill made him sweet but knocked him out. Pick your poison.*

Dad's back – the father I grew up with, whom my mother struggled with her whole married life. The controlling man who doles out approval based on what you do for him.

He was gone for a while. In his place was a sweet, happy man who loved everyone, including me. He was delighted to see me and also willing to let me go. He was friendly and appreciative.

Now, he barely acknowledges me when I arrive, his way of letting me know I've been away too long. He grumbles if I talk to or help others or if others join us. The minute I arrive, he begins to strategize how he can leave with me instead of enjoying our time together. And when I tell him I must leave, he gets angry and demanding.

I question the nurses as to whether his medication has changed or if it is possible he has developed a tolerance to Zoloft. I am disappointed to be told there are no apparent medical reasons why his nasty behavior has returned.

My mother used to tell me that she had to ask for help in Florida to leave him at the end of her visit – and tonight, I have to do the same. An aide comes to try to talk him down.

"You don't love me," he shouts at me. "Go on, leave. Leave!"

"We had a nice picnic, Dad, didn't we?" I ask, reverting back to the young girl still seeking his approval.

"No, we didn't."

Dad's back.

Not Tonight

I can't go to see my father tonight. I'm so tired and stressed out. He was so nasty and unpleasant last night that it felt just awful. He treats me as he treated my mother. Mean, demanding, withholding of any pleasantries. Controlling me to make me stay – and thereby driving me away. The cycle starts again.

Then Comes the Morning

Early the next morning before work, I go to visit my father and watch the little man sleeping soundly – with clenched fists.

I stroke his soft, white hair. And when he hears my voice, he wakes up and says, "I love you" and smiles at me with tears already in his eyes.

Substitute

"I LOVE YOU! I LOVE YOU, GOD DAMN IT! I LOVE YOU MORE THAN ANYTHING! BUT YOU DON'T LOVE ME!"

He screams his love to me, looking belligerent. I ask him not to yell at me. He says OK, and tries to smile, but soon starts right back in again. He obviously can't help it.

I sit despondent, realizing once again that I have stepped into my mother's life. He yells at me the way he yelled at her. Always demanding more, competing with the rest of her life, which she wasn't supposed to have. And apparently neither am I.

As I encourage him to eat something, he responds with disdain, "Oh, you're just like…." And he either dares not say or cannot remember my mother's name.

I feel angry and stop trying to cajole him. He begins to sob, sitting there in his yellow hat, with matching shirt, pants and socks.

When he realizes I'm crying too, he tries to cheer me up.

"Don't cry, honey. Don't. I'm OK." He feigns a smile.

I don't know how to help him; I can barely help myself.

"Where's my wife?" he asks.

"You know, Daddy. She's in heaven."

"Oh, I'm sorry," he says and starts to cry again.

No wonder he is angry. She left him, just like she left me.

Misdirected

I am angry with my mother – angry that she got sick and died and left me in this mess. Left me so bereft and devoid of any reserves. Left me to take care of my father – a sad, pathetic yet demanding man. Left me at odds with my only sister.

She always said not to worry, that everything always works out. Well, this didn't. My only disappointment in the relationship was her final and most cruel act – dying and leaving me to find my way alone.

I realize now that I was angry at the disease that stole her from me and that stole her life from her.

Battle Scars

"You lost yourself," Billy correctly observed. "You gave yourself over to caregiving. It's time to take care of yourself – spiritually – so that you can discover who you are now."

I sometimes wonder why I am still so bereft over losing my mother, besides the obvious of missing her. Then I remember what a slow, painful process her dying was for both of us. Watching her suffer was pure torture; the battle for her life not unlike a war. Yet there awaited another soldier fighting for his life whom I then had to rush off to care for.

Hospice tells me I am experiencing a form of post-traumatic stress disorder. That makes sense; my flashbacks feel as real as any veteran's. Meanwhile, my wounds go untreated since they are invisible to the naked eye. But I am bleeding all the same.

Night Shift

I am exhausted, leaving work at 8 p.m. I just want to go home. But I have not seen my father in two days so duty calls.

I find him sleeping in bed. The nurse tells me he had waited up a long time for me but then got tired. I take off my suit jacket, and he opens his eyes. He shakes with joy at my presence. I lie down next to him, as he scoots over to make room. We talk, and he tries hard to express himself, to be understood, but without much success. But I can clearly understand his frequent expressions of endearment: "I love you, honey. I love you!" He kisses my cheek and arm. We laugh at nothing in particular.

I sit him up, and he eats three cookies and his protein drink. We watch *Animal Planet* on television. At 9 p.m., I tell him I have to go, something we both dread.

"No," he says sadly but seemingly resigned. I promise I'll be back tomorrow, and I leave him alone, still munching and watching baseball.

I will be back tomorrow. But I'm so glad we had tonight.

Disappearing

I disappear from my father's sight, sometimes for two days at a time. I appear at will, we spend time together, and then I leave, disappearing beyond the locked door.

He watches me go, his eyes focused on me until I am out of sight. I watch him too as I move further away from him.

Sometimes, when he can no longer see me, I peer at him through the little glass window in the door. I see him trying to figure out what he should do next, and I imagine he wonders when I might reappear, before I disappear again all too soon.

Anticipated Loss

"I love you too much. That's the problem," he states with his head in his hands.

"Why is that a problem, Dad?" I ask. "I love you too."

"Because you might leave me, and then I'll be all alone."

"I'll never leave you, Dad," I promise, secretly wondering if I can keep that promise or if I am tempting fate.

"Yes, but you do leave me," he says, correct in his observation.

"But I always come back, Dad. Even when we get mad at each other, I always come back."

"OK," he says obviously relieved.

As I later tuck him into bed, he says, "I don't want to leave you, but sometimes I have to go to sleep."

"I know, Dad. It's OK," I respond, wondering what the future portends for each and both of us.

Nicholas

Although he has not had a nap, my dad is perky and excited when I pick him up late in the afternoon to take him to a dentist who has so kindly accepted him as a "new" patient at 89 years of age.

In the car, he asks me questions about this new dentist and wants to know how far away his office is. I tell him that Dr. Liberatore is a nice man who will help his teeth feel better. I tell him we aren't traveling far.

With his walker, we make our way into the office where the staff is awaiting this new patient's arrival. They call him Nicholas, and they make him feel like a celebrity. And Nicholas plays the part. He plops down in the big overstuffed couch to wait his turn, announcing that he is ready when the doctor is.

Dr. Liberatore offers a warm greeting and explains what he is going to do. Although it is obvious that Nicholas doesn't understand it all, Dr. Liberatore speaks directly to him out of respect. He checks the bite and makes adjustments accordingly.

I sit nearby, so proud of my father. He is attentive, cooperative, and polite. His eyes sparkle with playfulness. He opens and closes, taps and clamps, narrowly missing Dr. Liberatore's fingers a few times. (It's hard to tell if this is intentional or not, as both are starting to get a little silly.) Hygienists start gathering to check out this model patient with a good sense of humor.

"How does that feel?" Dr. Liberatore asks upon completion of the process.

"Beau-ti-ful," Nicholas responds with animation. "Beau-ti-ful!"

On the return trip, we share a root beer. He says he is tired so I put him to bed as soon as we get back. While tucking him in, I ask to see his teeth. He complies with a big toothy grin.

"They look great," I say.

"I know," he says. "I really like that guy."

"He likes you too," I respond. And with that happy thought, my father closes his eyes for a well-deserved rest, his teeth good as new.

Nicholas II

I am unable to accompany my father to his follow up dental appointment so I call for a report. Michelle tells me he did great, that he cheered up the whole office, as it had been a particularly challenging day. "Dr. Liberatore needed him especially today," she says. "Nicholas really helped him a lot."

Dr. Liberatore calls me later that day to tell me his staff was reflecting on the trials and tribulations of their relatively new dental practice. As consolation, one of them said, "What if we had never met Nicholas? What a shame that would have been!"

My heart swells with pride to think that my father – my often-difficult father – is considered such a joy by these professionals.

There is no doubt that taking care of my father – having full responsibility for him – is difficult and at times a burden. But I have had benefit of the most amazing experiences a daughter could have by being present for him as he reaches his full potential of humanity.

> Dr. Liberatore and his receptionist visited my father at the end of his life. They told me he said he was scared – he never said that to me.

The Best Lunch

I arrive to have lunch with my dad not knowing how I will find him: asleep, awake, nasty, sad, demanding? My trepidation mounts as I approach, and I am aware that I always feel a sense of uncertainty as I walk down his hallway.

Today, he is happy to see me. I take him from the dining room to the private conference table.

"Do you like soup?" I ask and am delighted by his response. He starts eagerly eating that and all the other food I have brought.

"I like this. I'm happy," he says with a big grin.

Gratitude fills my soul. He is eating and happy! Staff come in for various reasons, and he offers them the mangled deviled eggs in his hand. He grins and laughs with them.

A package arrives from my sister, full of political memorabilia. I try on the hat, and he claps his hands saying, "You look so cute in that. Now I want you to keep it!" I tell him repeatedly it is a gift for him, but he insists I take it. "I'm so happy now that you have that," he says.

He asks if I have to leave and accepts my all-too-familiar answer. He remains cheery as I wheel him back.

I am no longer naïve as to what inevitably awaits us. But today, my joy in being able to share this miraculous interlude is unbridled. *Thank you, God.*

Dining "Out"

"We're going to have a nice dinner tonight, Dad," I tell him. "Get dressed up so we can go to a nice place."

His face lights up, a face that had enjoyed many a night out once upon a time. "Really?" he asks.

"Really," I respond.

When I arrive later, he is indeed dressed up, in his cream-colored sweater and cap. "Are we going now?" he asks. And off we go. Down the hall. Down the hall to the nursing home dining room, a place he eats twice a day.

"Is *this* where we're going?" he asks.

I read disappointment into that question and wonder if I have unfairly misled him. But my hesitancy is short-lived. For the dining room has been transformed into an elegant restaurant as surely as Cinderella's pumpkin had become a coach. And employees have been transformed into wait staff.

The maitre d' seats us at a table for four in this room with soft lights and music. Within minutes, a waitress offers us faux beer or wine from "the bar." My dad beams. Wine! We clink glasses and toast. He smiles and says, "This is nice." Two glasses later, the salad and rolls. No need to worry about his fluid intake tonight.

Slowly the tables fill up, with most families sporting at least one wheelchair. Family members assemble, all dressed up in order to recreate once more that feeling of having a normal outing with their loved one. Couples dine at tables for two, as independent spouses join their infirm partners for a normal meal together. And slowly, residents are transformed back into people with normal lives. This feels right to them; this feels normal.

The main entrée is delivered, and I hold my breath as to whether my dad and I will have our typical struggle over food. Not tonight. Tonight he picks up his fork and independently eats pork roast, potatoes and carrots. "This is good," he says. A wave of relief sweeps over me, for I too need and want this night to feel normal. He cleans his plate. No need to worry about his caloric intake tonight.

Dessert follows, and my dad sips from a real teacup for the

first time in years. He remembers how to do it. And I remember watching him do it in what seems like an eternity ago.

Tonight, I catch a glimpse of my dad's former lifestyle. Eating in restaurants, drinking wine, flirting with waitresses. But more importantly, he had the chance to feel normal again. Just down the hall. Yet a lifetime ago.

Proud of You

> "Will you remember me?" he asked.
> "How could I ever forget you?" I responded with
> all sincerity.

"I'm proud of you, Dad," I tell him. "You've done so well. You've really made the most of your new life. People like you. You're fun to be with. You're a wonderful man, Dad. Thank you."

"Thank you," he responds with a grin and a look that suggests he's never heard such praise before. And I never thought I'd be able to honestly say such words to him. But today, I am surprised and delighted to be able to say and mean them.

The Forgotten

I recognize her voice instantly. On the other end of the line is a doctor who cared for my mother when she was in the hospital. A very busy doctor who I hadn't seen in over eight months. A very busy doctor who is taking the time to call a deceased patient's daughter.

Just moments before, I was lamenting the seeming disappearance of people who cared about my mother (and indirectly about me). The people who forgot to remember. People who said they'd stay in touch, people who said they'd miss her and would never forget her, people with the best of intentions to remain connected, had vanished from my life. People we used to see every day, people who became deeply involved in the most intimate details of our lives, were gone. There was limited outreach or contact; I remained alone in my grief.

Life just goes on, I philosophized. *People move on.* My mother was indeed unforgettable…if only for a while. But apparently, the gaping hole she left had already been filled for some.

And then, the phone rings. "I've been thinking about you and your mother so much," the doctor says in her elegant accent. "I cried when I heard she had died. I have pictures of her in her hat at the hospital."

There it is – out of the blue! The comfort I need and well-deserved redemption for my mother. More than ever, at this point in time, I need to know that people still care, that my mother was not just a fleeting blip on the monitor. That she lingers in others' memories as she does in mine. That it's not all over…just because she died.

This remarkable doctor breathed new life into my mother's spirit by caring enough to remember the potentially forgotten. The call was consistent with her exceptional approach to health care, infused with passion and intuition. Hers was the face – the beautiful face – my mother woke up to every day. Her warm eyes and smile gave my mother much comfort and reassurance during very desperate times, and I believe added months to her life. And maybe to mine as well.

> *Years later, I located Dr. Misalati in Maryland. She told me she has since given birth to a daughter, whom she hopes will someday sit at her bedside as I did for my mother.*

Sunday

My mom called every Sunday night. Sometimes I
dreaded the call because it interrupted my plans. And
sometimes I'd feel guilty for missing the call.

The day looms long and empty. A day full of potential for me to get things done. Yet it also stands as a mockery to my inertia, my inability to tackle what needs to be done.

It is another day without my mother – another day further away from her passing to solidify the permanence. Here's another day when I again won't hear from her. Another day that she is gone.

When your parent first dies, you get a lot of attention from others. She and you become celebs, and people are willing to listen to your story. They help you keep her alive for a while. But before too long, you become one more person whose mother is dead. Nothing special – it happens to all of us.

The rain that comes Sunday afternoon is a welcome backdrop to my grieving – which is all I am able to do on Sunday.

Years after her death, I still expected to hear from her
on Sunday, and so regret those calls I missed. And I still
reached for the phone to call her.

Part Twelve: May God Have Mercy

May God Have Mercy

"I'll walk you down to the door, OK?" he asked from his
wheelchair. "Or do you want me to walk you all the way
to your car?"

Their wheelchairs are all lined up on the first floor, headed toward the elevator. They are motionless sitting there, as if in a stopped bus.

"Where are you going?" I cheerfully ask them, as I make my way to the other elevator.

"Wherever they put us," a woman accurately responds.

"May God have mercy on us," another refrains.

I hop onto the elevator with no response. What is there to say to their candor? I arrive at my dad's floor and find that he too is lined up in the hallway.

"For me?" he asks the aide in disbelief, pointing to me. "For me?"

He is one of many people on that floor who are watching the door, just hoping that it will produce a visitor "for" them.

I whisk him off, for today he is the lucky one. This visitor is "for" him.

May God have mercy.

Old People Can't

Old people can't take care of old people.

They don't have the stamina, strength, or energy to do what
has to be done.

To bring them food, drag laundry, push their wheelchairs.

To drive the distance, to answer late night phone calls.

To make sound medical decisions, to stay on top of health
insurance issues.

To bear up under the strain of another old person.

Old people can't.

How much longer can I?

Did You, Mama?

*Did you die just so this wouldn't be your life? I see the old women
– physically and emotionally exhausted – wheeling their husbands
around in their wheelchairs. That would have been no life for you.*

*We always asked you not to die first, and you even promised that
you wouldn't. I believed you had that kind of power and control.
Did you, Mama?*

*You did get Dad settled in a nursing facility in Florida before
you got sick so we wouldn't have to make that decision. You mod-
eled the needed advocacy and your wishes for his care, leaving me a
guide to take care of the man you loved so much, despite (or maybe
because of) it all.*

*But did you die just so this wouldn't be your life? Did you,
Mama? If so, I understand.*

Dad's Life

I arrive at lunchtime and find him sipping his coffee, food untouched. He has a sparkle in his eyes as he flirts with the aide and the other women at his table. He greets me in an exaggerated animated fashion.

The aide tells me he has many "girlfriends," and I tell her that has always been the case, much to my mother's chagrin. One of his fellow residents tells me, "We're all just crazy about him." I am delighted to hear that he has a life in between my visits.

I take him to the TV room, give him a non-alcoholic beer and turn on the football game. He grins and eats the snacks I brought. Too soon I tell him I have to leave.

"No," he says. "Why do you always have to go?"

I tell him I have work to do, and he responds, "You always do that – you always run off."

His accurate assessment stings. I do "run off" and leave him. In fact, I suspect he is on alert to listen for the jingle of my car keys from the minute I arrive.

As the door slams and locks behind me, I watch him through the window as he begins to re-engage with others, back to his real life without me.

All I Have

I sat next to a geriatric doctor on a flight back from Tampa during those months of commuting. He was on his way to give a lecture to medical students about end-of-life care. "Is the end of life always shitty?" I blurt out. "Yes," he bluntly replies. "It is for almost everyone. We don't want to accept that, but it's true." "Then I want to die like Princess Di," I hear myself respond.

He is content watching golf on TV with me. Until the aide comes in to "change" him, at my request.

"Leave me be, please. I just want to be with my daughter right now," he pleads. Suddenly, his afternoon is out of control as they roll and wipe him, stripping him of his pride and dignity.

His lunch tray is then brought to him in bed. He refuses any and all options I offer, saying, "Please, dear. I don't want that. Please!"

I get annoyed and threaten to leave, a trick my mother always pulled. He says he is sorry, but he still refuses to eat. It is the only control he can exert; yet I still try to deprive him of that as well.

Have I not yet learned that nurturing is more important than nourishment?

Sobbing with frustration, he looks around his nursing home room and says, "This is all I have…all I have."

Like a Statue

> *A waiter told me his grandmother used to tell him, "As I am now, so shall you be."*

Mary, with her jet black hair, walks into the little room where I am sitting with my dad. She tells us to watch out for Athlete's Foot in the shower and to not leave valuables around. She is animated and speaks with great authority, so I assume she is a new employee. We tell her we will be careful. She then tells us to watch out for Athlete's Foot in the shower and to not leave valuables around. And then, tells us once more before leaving.

I follow her out and am told that Mary used to work on that floor. And now she is a patient.

As I am now, so shall you be.

Mary soon enough realized she was no longer in charge. "This is no life," she told me. "I sit here like a statue, and no one even looks at me." She went on to say how depressed she was, having nothing to look forward to, and how cruel others could be. I rubbed her back and said, "I understand." But I truly couldn't even begin to imagine how desperately lonely Mary and her counterparts must have been.

Those People

Those people used to mean nothing to me. I didn't even know or care that they existed. Oh sure, I'd see them outside the "facility" when I happened to walk by. Walk by and never stop to chat. Walk by too afraid of some of the deformities and disabilities that were all too obvious. Yes, I'd walk by, so glad that I didn't have to stop. So glad that it was they who were infirm and I had no stake, no responsibility for them. They were just those people – pitiful indeed, but not my problem.

Then one of my people ended up in there. In that facility. One of my people needed round-the-clock care and had to go live with those people. I knew he wasn't like those people, but he still needed a supervised place to live like they did.

So when I visited my father, I'd walk past all those people. My dad just happened to be there – but we didn't have to have relationships with those people. We were different.

But slowly, those people became *these* people. I got to know their names, their stories, their families. I got to see the underbelly of the nursing home, the inner workings of residents struggling to maintain their independence while in an institution. Those people are now *my* people, people no different than I except for one accident, illness, or year of birth. Those people have shown me that we are all *one* people. And that *those* people no longer exist.

The Birthday Party

Parties in nursing homes aren't traditional parties. Residents can't do party stuff – most can't move of their own volition. They wait for a party to happen, and then they sit and watch.

My dad is doing just that; the man who used to make parties happen singlehandedly is idly sitting at a table. I easily spot him, dressed in his matching bright pink hat, shirt and pants.

He didn't know that I too would be attending Julia's 100th birthday party. When he sees me, he lights up with a big grin and waves. We hug, hold hands, sing, eat cake and drink punch. We kick our legs to *New York, New York*. At my request, the disc jockey plays *Volare* and dedicates it to Nick. He grins.

Soon the party is over, and I must return to work. He says, "Goodbye. I love you," and I watch my father disappear into the elevator with an aide.

There to Help

I help my father out of the car and into his wheelchair. As we head for the ramp, I can see her little face through the storm door. I wonder what the neighbor girl is doing in my house. Nonetheless, there she is, seven-year-old Elizabeth.

Peter and I have been dreading this holiday since losing our mothers. It is our first Easter with just our fathers, and it is to be only four of us "celebrating." We hadn't counted on Elizabeth.

When asked, she tells me she is there to help. "Help do what?" I ask. "Serve you," she announces. I tell her that is certainly very nice but not necessary. In response, she simply picks up the cheese platter and offers it to the two elderly men already seated at the table. She silently checks them out and is obviously uncomfortable around them. She does not interact with them, and they do not engage her at all. As I see them through her eyes, they seem rather scary and humorless. Two grumpy nonagenarians.

After a while, she tests the waters. She begins to do pratfalls, and both men tell her to be careful. Because this got their attention, her falls become more dramatic, her laughter more infectious. I leave the dining room to get the main course and when I return, her Barbie is sitting on my 98 year old father-in-law's shoulder, and my 90-year-old father has a purple gauze bag on his head. She asks us to take her picture with each of them looking quite ridiculous. She starts imitating my father and sneaking up behind him to scare him. She tells my father-in-law to "stop being so serious and start laughing more." She dubs them "Pops" and "Bucko" interchangeably, and the old geezers grin from ear to ear.

"I don't think we're getting along at all, do you?" she asks them, giggling. She insists on sharing her Easter candy with them, doling out the jellybeans one by one. But that is the least of her generosity.

Before too long, my father retires to the couch. She sings him a lullaby and quietly plays his childhood game of marbles nearby as he snores. She keeps her eye on him, and the minute he wakes up, she jumps up and hugs him. "Grandpa!" she exclaims and, although very tired, he smiles at her warmly. Her face falls, however, when he asks to return to the nursing home to rest. She gets his wheelchair, walks with us to the car, kisses him goodbye, and waves as we drive off.

"She's nice," my father comments as he waves back at her. "Will you bring her to see me sometime?" I promise I will. "Good," he responds. "Good."

That evening, I call Elizabeth's mother to express appreciation for loaning us her daughter all day. She replies, "Oh, we were afraid she might be bothering you, but she told us that you needed her help."

Elizabeth was right – although we had not asked, we did need her help. Help remembering that life goes on, that humor transcends generations, and that it's good to be silly no matter your age. And even though Dryphuss ended up with sticky marshmallows on his silky fur and the rug took a beating, Elizabeth helped in ways that she cannot yet understand, and we could not have possibly foreseen.

Moving Day

My dad and I sit outside the nursing home, snacking and watching the comings and goings. Soon we see a cart loaded with furniture leaving the building, headed for a pick-up truck.

How nice, I thought. *Someone's going home.* I see my father intently watching too and wonder what he's thinking. Out loud I say to him, "Looks like someone's moving."

"Yes," he replies. "Look at all that stuff."

I then realize that only the possessions are going home. And I hear another resident quietly mumble to herself, "Looks like we lost another one."

Mothers' Day

The first Mothers' Day without my mother. It's hard. But no harder than every day without her.

I take my father party snacks for dinner, like the appetizers I used to serve when my parents would visit. My mother is obviously absent though, and my dad asks, "Is she ever coming back, or is she gone for good?"

"She's gone for good," I tell him.

But I don't really believe that. *She's with us, Dad. She's all around us,* I want to say. But he's confused enough...as am I.

As the day draws to a close, I am sad – but no more today than yesterday or tomorrow.

Happy Mothers' Day, Mom. I love you. And I'm glad you were not in a nursing home today. It's better where you are. But...are you EVER coming back?

Dad's Birthday

"It's your dad's birthday next week. What are we going to do?"

Although it was October, my mother was obsessed with needing to make plans for her husband's birthday. I tried to tell her Dad's birthday wasn't until May, but it didn't matter. She wanted to make sure she didn't miss it.

But today, she did miss it. Today, my dad celebrates his 90th birthday without his wife. I throw him a party with other nursing home residents, but it doesn't mean much. He is weak and incoherent, as are most of the guests.

I wish we had celebrated Dad's birthday with my mother last fall. So what if it wasn't time yet? It was the only time she had left. And today we "celebrate" after she is gone. But just barely.

Graveside Visit

Without a doubt, I think I'll be able to find the site. Even though there is not yet a headstone, I am sure I wouldn't ever forget the spot where my mother was put into the ground. But I search in vain, crying to the heavens, *I'm here, Mama. Where are you? Do you see me? I know you are here somewhere, but I can't find you. I guess it doesn't matter because you're not really here anyway. But I want you to know that I am.*

My mother never visited her mother's grave. She told me she didn't believe in doing that because her mother is not there. She told me not to go to her grave site either. *Dust to dust, ashes to ashes,* she'd quote. But I am still here, searching.

Responsible

I go away for the weekend – one lousy weekend – and upon my return, find out my father has fallen again. "But he didn't get hurt," the staff assure me, just as they did when he broke his hip.

Yet, when I see him, his knees are swollen and bruised. The stories differ as to how he fell, yet there is not much to be gained by chasing down the real story. Because that's what happens at 90 – you simply give way, quite suddenly. He is weak; he is fragile. He now needs two people to assist him.

I can't help but feel responsible. After all, I didn't see him for three days, the longest I've left him since my mother's funeral.

They tell me he did not eat much and was despondent and crabby in my absence. Great.

Now that I'm back, he is eating and happy, albeit weak.

So, I must be the one keeping him alive. I am his touchstone, giving him hope and a reason to keep going. I leave and things literally fall apart.

"You were away," he says to me in a somewhat accusatory tone. (Or do I imagine that?)

I was away, yes. And you fell. And I feel responsible, damn it.

Spirit Circle

I sit in the spirit circle in my backyard early in the morning, feeling so desperate. Visiting my mother's grave over the weekend left a lingering sadness that I can't shake. I sit intending to send my father reiki but feel devoid of any strength or power to do so. I know I am the one who needs reinforcement right now. All I can do is sit and sob.

As I sit with my eyes closed, I feel the presence of others. I see the outline of my mother, visible against bright light. She leads the others, with a headdress on. One by one, my deceased relatives enter the circle. They all crowd into the little space, and I feel their power, their warmth, their energy. I say a prayer to them:

> *You are all so much wiser and stronger than I because*
> *you have completed your earthly journeys. I know that*
> *God is in every one of you, as he is in me, and you have*
> *brought God to me. Help me to find the wisdom and*
> *strength to carry on your work on this earthly plane.*

We all bow our heads for a while, warm in the light my ancestors project. I continue to sit there feeling stronger and wiser. Within seconds, my visitors leave, and chimes begin to ring out from behind me. The music lasts for several seconds, during which I try to convince myself that I am hallucinating. But I am sure I hear it loud and clear. When it ends, I turn around to identify the source, but there is no one and nothing there. They have all left.

My Day Off

I took a day off from work today to catch up on my life. It begins with an 8:30 a.m. phone call: The doctor has made a referral to Hospice in response to my inquiry as to my father's prognosis.

Now we await word as to whether my father is deemed eligible to die within six months. Again.

A subsequent call to the nursing home reveals my father is grumpy and slapped a drink out of a woman's hand. I race up to find him scared and dejected – and refusing food. So I take him out to breakfast, where he is upbeat and quite articulate.

"You look like you've been working very hard," he says to me. "But this is what makes me happiest – being with you."

When I take him back, he is sullen again. "Your father is very lucky to have you. I mean *very* lucky," another resident tells me.

"I'm lucky to have him too," I respond, my eyes filling with tears, my precious free hours having been eaten up.

When I approach the social worker and head nurse about ways to address his despondency, they look at me as if I have two heads and say, "You can't have it both ways. Do you want Hospice involved, or do you want us to keep him active and healthy?"

I tell them I know that is not the dichotomy Hospice sets up, that you can have both. I tell them my father and I need more support, and I start to cry. I turn to leave, and they let me.

Perhaps my advocacy is working against my dad; perhaps they

resent my interference. Nonetheless, my day is shot from the hours this intervention took, in trying to help my dad survive until he dies.

When and how can I carve out a space for myself? I am desperate for the time to find myself again, amidst the rubble of my life.

Although he would be dead four months later, my father did not qualify for Hospice services at this time.

Alone

He is so little in his bed and so delighted to see me. He moves over as best he can to make room and offers me all the food I just brought him.

We watch TV, and then I too soon start to leave, promising to return tomorrow.

"What time?" he asks, as if it mattered. As if he could still tell time.

He is so forlorn, but resigned to yet another departure. "I miss you so much," he cries. "See you tomorrow."

As I leave, I am frightened by the thought that no one is intimately concerned about his care but me. There is no one to call to update, no one anxiously waiting to hear from me about his condition. My sister chooses to call the staff rather than me.

We are alone. We are both alone, Dad.

Live 'Til You Die

I have been angry with my mother and disappointed that she didn't show me how to die. I expected her to be braver, to accept her fate more readily. After all, she was such a devout woman.

Instead she was afraid and showed it, openly despondent. That wasn't the way I thought this remarkable woman would go out.

Tonight, a phone call from Billy helps. He reminisces fondly about time spent with my mother – how gentle and gracious she always was, despite her desperate situation. How loving and open she was toward others, despite the pain she felt.

"I miss those times with her. You created such a remarkable end-of-life experience for her…and yourself," he says.

While I miss my mother, I never thought about missing "those times." They were the scariest days of my life to date. But perhaps my mother did teach me more about dying than I realize. While she fought death, she never fought me or other caregivers. She didn't get bitter or blame the world for what befell her. She railed against the disease but was pleasant to others, despite her physical and psychological pain.

Billy later follows up our conversation with an email. He writes that my mother railed against death because she loved living. She grasped every opportunity to live life – even if crying were all she could do to show she was still alive. "She used it all up before she left. That's how we should die – living until our last breath is drawn," he writes.

Who am I to judge how another approaches death? My mother deserves way more credit than I have been giving her. I guess I wanted her to make it easier for me by accepting her fate. The fact that she fought for her life is to be admired, not resented. Instead of showing me how to die, she showed me how to live.

Bad Things Happen

> *"Bad things happen in clusters," I told Letitia. "Do good things happen in clusters too?" she asked rhetorically. Probably – but we tend not to notice.*

"There's not much we can do at this stage," the veterinarian tells us. In a surreal moment, we are told we will soon be losing Dryphuss to cancer.

We have no capacity to absorb this information. *When it rains, it pours* is not just a clever adage anymore.

In response to more bad news about my life, friends try to help but say stupid things:

"Bad things happen in threes (or multiples thereof)."

"Maybe it's good you're getting all your grieving done at once."

"It might be good that this is happening when you are already so down that you couldn't get much lower."

"God doesn't give you any more than you can handle."

Oh, really? Then tell him to leave Dryphuss the hell alone because I can't handle yet another loss.

We Didn't Know

I am crying in my backyard when a neighbor appears with her dog. I tell her that Peter and I both lost our mothers, and now our dog is dying. I am feeling desperate for comfort, but this I don't say.

"Oh, I'm so sorry," she says. "We didn't know. Everything seemed normal over there. We just didn't know."

"That's OK," I respond. For how were they to know? You can't see loss and depression and despair from the outside of a house. Things looked "normal" at our place, I imagine.

Homes look happy with lights on; they seem warm and cozy. And they belie the darkness that occupants may feel in their hearts.

Forgiveness

The Bereavement Group facilitator asks us to write a letter to our deceased loved one. I don't believe I have anything left to say. Then this pours out.

> Dear Mom,
>
> I forgive you for getting sick, for faltering, for being weak and scared. It wasn't what I expected, and I felt betrayed and abandoned when it happened. I thought you'd show me how to be brave and strong. I thought you'd show me how to die. Instead I saw how vulnerable and afraid you were. It scared me.
>
> Forgive me my desperation, my inability to accept the inevitable. Forgive me for not recognizing sooner how sick you were and for leaving you alone too long. Forgive me for not being totally honest with you about your condition. Forgive me for feeding you instead of holding you.
>
> I love you so much. You are deep in my soul always. Thank you for the inspiration, the unconditional love, and the role modeling.
>
> > Patty

Mercy Dying

> In the past, my mother was frequently heard to say, "Life at any cost is not living; it is merely existing."

As I leave my father's nursing home, I overhear a very debilitated resident complain, "You wouldn't treat a dog like this!"

The all-too-apparent truth is that dying is often a prolonged, painful process that we force humans to endure while sparing our pets the same agony.

My mother and my dog died within six months of each other. Both were sources of unconditional love and comfort for me. And sadly, both developed cancer. I witnessed each as they refused food, slowly lost functioning, and eventually died. As blasphemous as it sounds, my mother and my dog were both very hard to lose, a truism only those who have known the love of a dog could understand.

There is one big difference, however. I was able to end my dog's life when it became apparent that there was no hope, no cure. I was unable to do any such humane act to spare my beloved mother prolonged agony. And now I live with that contradiction.

My mother suffered for over nine months with a debilitating brain tumor, paralyzed and totally dependent on others. Despite months of treatment, the doctors declared that there was no hope, and she would just have to wait it out until death intervened. Today, I am left with the horrific flashbacks of her suffering and pain, both physical and psychological. And that one fleeting conversation we had about euthanasia.

With Dryphuss, we were told it would only be a matter of weeks. But through some alternative treatments, we bought him another three months. Until…he stopped eating and started groaning. All the symptoms were aligned with the inevitability of an imminent death and an inability to save his life. We took him back to the veterinarian's office to assess whether we could manage his pain or should end his suffering. After a lengthy, personalized, physical and psychological consult, the vet determined that since Dryphuss was not going to get better, we were putting him (and ourselves) through unnecessary suffering and trauma. His quality of life was not good, and he had lost all doggie joie de vivre. More or different medication might buy us a few days, but his time was drawing nigh.

"I'm not ready yet," I selfishly told the vet. "I just need one more day with him."

"I love people who don't give up," the sympathetic vet replied. "But the problem with people who don't give up is that they don't know *when* to give up. Dryphuss is suffering – it's time to let him go."

I nodded in acquiescence. I loved Dryphuss enough to do what was best for him. After a very tearful goodbye and desperate clinging hugs, we allowed him to leave through the compassionate act of euthanasia. Afterward, his pain was gone, and he was at peace.

Friends tried to console me by telling me how loving an act it was, how kind a gesture to end his suffering while he still had his dignity. I keep thinking how paradoxical it is that I was able to access "humane" euthanasia for my dog but not for my mother. What about *her* dignity??

I know the argument can be made that we had another three months with Dryphuss that we wouldn't have had if we had ended his life prematurely, obviously drawing parallels with what could have happened to my mother were euthanasia an option. My response would be that we *didn't* put Dryphuss down prematurely. Through well-reasoned and well-researched decision-making, coupled with unconditional love, we knew when it was time…and didn't do it one minute too soon for his sake or ours. The veterinarian and family decided to let him go when it became apparent there was no hope.

I am new to contemplating the implications of euthanasia for humans. My recent back-to-back losses have provided a new lens through which to view assisted suicide. The abortion debate raises the question, "When does life begin?" I find myself wondering, "When does life end?"

Death of a Marriage

"Do you think we're being punished?" I asked Peter.

Our 23 year marriage is ending – it cannot sustain the multiple blows incurred in such a short period of time. Our mothers and our dog have passed. We both now care for ailing fathers. I am exhausted and resentful. He is too.

When my mother died, I lost my cheerleader, the one who unconditionally believed in me and encouraged me. She gave me strength, like Samson's hair. Perhaps I have become too needy, but these losses have left a void between Peter and me that is too big to fill.

Death has eaten a hole in our relationship. If I am to be lonely, I'd rather be alone.

Tired of Myself

People must be getting tired of me.
I'm tired of myself.
My shitty life, my vigilance, my self-righteousness.
My pathetic pity party.

I'm tired of my story.
My embarrassingly lonely story.
I know my mama's heart must be breaking as she watches
     what's become of my life.
She would not want me to sacrifice my life for anyone.

I believe she is leading me to the questions as well as to the answers.

But it sure doesn't make it any easier.

Help Me to Understand

Help me to understand.
To understand where I've been and where I'm going.
To understand who I am and what I want.
To understand my pain, fear, and loss.
To understand why my whole world fell apart, beginning innocuously enough with one broken hip.
Help me to understand why I don't understand.

Stupid Little Bear

As I walk into the last meeting of the Daughters' Bereavement Group, there are a dozen little Gund bears sitting on a table. I instantly know they must be for us and also know I don't want or need a stupid little bear.

The white teddy bears are all very fancy, dressed in brightly colored knit sweaters and hats. The Hospice facilitators tell us that a local volunteer group donated them to help console those grieving the loss of a loved one. We are each asked to choose one.

Reluctantly, I play along, choosing one with a pink and purple sweater and a hat with a pom-pom. I note that I chose it as reminiscent of my mother's fashion sense. But I still know it's silly – kids' stuff – and I don't care if I have one or not; I chose one simply as a courtesy.

I even leave the stupid little bear in my car for a few days. And then the transference begins to take place. Her warm brown eyes seem to look at me with the intensity of understanding. She is sweet and unassuming, offering silent comfort in a way I never expected. She is soft and cuddly.

I begin to feel warmth and love from this bear – to accept her as a surrogate source of unconditional love. She needs me, and I need her. I hug her to my chest.

I thank the little bear for giving me something I didn't know I needed – because I was too stupid to realize that she was not.

A small stuffed bear once more gave me comfort as
another bear had half a century before.

Don't Show Me Pumpkins

Don't show me pumpkins.
Not yet.
Don't show me red and yellow leaves.
I'm not ready.
Don't show me fall fashions.
I'm not interested.

It can't be fall yet.
Another summer can't be gone.
I couldn't have lost yet another summer.
Where did it go?
Where did I go?

Don't show me pumpkins.
I still need watermelons.

Trick or Treat

I am annoyed with my father for being so rude to the little trick-or-treaters who come through his unit; he selfishly doesn't want to give up the candy he was given to distribute.

Although I say nothing, he picks up on it.

"I know you're mad at me," he says. I admit that I am but then realize that there is no place for "mad" when time is short. He watches my face, and I turn on a smile and tell him everything's OK, he has nothing to worry about.

He so hopes that is true, and so do I.

Don't Leave Me

My dad and I watch the Notre Dame/Navy football game together today, something I would never have done in days gone by. But today, I did it for and with him. Or did I do it for myself?

As surely as the leaves turn color and fall to the ground, I know that my days with him are numbered. This time will not come again when I can be with my father. Too soon he will be gone. So while I still can, I will sit by his side, which is when he is most content.

"Don't leave me," he cries after the game. "Don't leave me."

"I have to," I respond. And silently wonder where I left my own life.

Tables Turned

A woman at the nursing home approaches me to say that she's been watching me interact with my father and was inspired to email her granddaughter about it.

All this time I have been recording my observations of others, I never once thought that I might be the subject of someone else's writing. *Someone is writing about me? I'm the one who is chroni-cling my desperate journey, not someone else!*

I tell her I am both honored and surprised, and I ask if she could forward me a copy. Within a few days, she presents me with a beautiful note about my dad and a copy of this email:

> *I was sitting up front with Grandma, listening to LOUD music. My eyes filled with tears at one particular scene. A daughter was with her father. I have seen the man many times – and I have seen her too. She requested the song* My Way *to be played for her father. As it was being played, she kneeled and rubbed his back to share the thoughts in the man's head as the song played. It's hard to describe what I saw – the song gave the man so much in those moments that it played. Then they played* New York, New York, *and his daughter took her father's feet off the rests on the wheel chair and told him to kick to the song – and she kicked her legs to the song also. I get a whole lot from the ones I meet at the nursing home.*

I vaguely remember that day, vaguely remember the interaction. But someone was watching, turning the tables on the person with the "little book."

A Book's Cover

My father's desperation is palpable, and so is mine. There is nothing to do, nothing to even talk about. I catch a glimpse of a custodian who my dad really likes and call him over to say hello, just to break the silence. My dad's face lights up when he sees Mike; in fact, they are genuinely glad to see each other, grinning and laughing as they shake hands.

Mike turns to me and asks if I am the one who wrote the story

in the newspaper about dancing with my father. I respond affirmatively. He indicates he'd like to read more of my material and
encourages me to submit my work more widely.

He continues to stand there, a bit awkward. I finally ask, although it seems a long shot, "Are *you* a writer, Mike?" After the
words are out, I immediately regret asking him. *He's a cleaner,
for Christ's sake!* But without hesitation, he confidently replies,
"Yes."

"Have you been published?" I ask incredulously. He tells me
he's written two books and has a third on the way.

I translate for my dad: "Mike writes books, Dad."

"What kind of books?" he asks even more surprised than I.
When I tell him humorous books, he laughs, points at Mike and
says, "He's good."

Mike smiles, says a warm goodbye, and goes back inside while
my dad and I eat our snack, a snack my father wouldn't touch before Mike took the time to cheer him up. Writer or not, he makes
a lasting difference in my dad's life every day.

My dad is then ready for a nap, so we head toward his room,
only to find Mike sweeping the floor, reminiscent of Cinderella
after the ball.

"I haven't quit my day job yet," he laments.

And I can't help but think how important it is to not judge a
book by its cover.

Just Not Right

> *"You're not afraid of anything!" he told me with a big
> grin after I "stole" a cup of coffee for him from the
> nurses' station because he thought it tasted better from
> there. He apparently did not know the terror I was
> feeling every waking moment...*

I show up 20 minutes late as usual. I find him fast asleep in his wheelchair in the hall, danish and coffee untouched.

"Hi, Daddy," I say.

No response.

"Dad!"

He continues to sleep as if he doesn't hear anything. Teardrops are evident in the corner of his right eye.

"He's been very unhappy," one of his fellow residents tells me. "He doesn't like sitting here."

Instant guilt followed by concern.

"Dad!" I shout in his face again.

He opens his eyes and gives a near-delirium smile, sweet but vacant. As I bustle about to get him ready to go outside, he starts weeping. Not his typical attention-seeking cry, but genuinely sad crying.

"What's the matter, Dad?" I ask as I hug him.

Through his weepy eyes, he responds, "I love you." I respond in-kind.

I invite him to come have coffee with me. His pasted-on smile returns so we move outside to the patio.

He looks at me and asks, "What's wrong with me?" I tell him I couldn't wake him. He nods and says, "I'm just not right."

He eats the deviled eggs I brought, and we sit and watch the birds. When he begins to doze again, I return him to bed. He smiles sweetly, and I promise to return tomorrow.

"You sure?" he asks. "What time?" as if wanting to make sure he is available.

I'm Sick

For two weeks, my father has been asking me to take him out to breakfast. I have put it off because it has become too hard for me to get him into restaurants. This morning, I finally call to make arrangements with the nurse.

She tells me he has a fever and isn't feeling well. I race over to find a very small, frail man sleeping. I wake him up, and his pale face briefly lights up with a smile. He then starts crying in my arms.

"I'm sick," he says. I climb into bed with him.

He is failing and failing rapidly. I am startled to see the warning signs are there. He won't eat or drink, his skin is translucent, and he perseverates. He calls for my mother and his deceased sister.

His cough is fierce; he is agitated and doesn't swallow.

I am losing my last parent.

Part Thirteen: That's Enough

That's Enough

> *"Don't try to play too many roles," the chaplain advised*
> *me. "Be his daughter, not his nurse. Just love him and*
> *provide comfort – don't try to get pills into him."*

He is refusing food and drink, rips off the oxygen, and spits out the antibiotic. The nurses continue to try to treat him, but he belligerently tells them, "No more" and "Get away" and "That's enough." I tell him he would get better if he takes the pills. He responds, "I don't care."

"I can't do this much longer, Dad," I tell him. He responds, "Neither can I." But when he notices I am crying, he says, "I'm all right, honey. I'm all right," not wanting to upset me further.

I repeatedly ask him, "Do you want to go to the hospital?" and he emphatically declines every time.

His distress intensifies, so I call for more morphine. The nurse tells me that the doctor is refusing to increase the dosage based on my dad's living will and says my father must go to the hospital for intravenous and possibly tube feeding. I panic remembering my mother's phone call from the Florida emergency room 18 months earlier.

Aides and nurses tell me that it would be more peaceful for him to die in his own room with those who have cared for him for 16 months. And having watched my mother-in-law die in a hospital, I vividly recall the difference between her final moments and my own mother's.

But what do I know?

I know that my father is dying.

The Living's Will

When they arrived in the mail ten years ago, I was surprised. Both parents had completed a living will naming me as their health care proxy. My mother's stipulated that she did not want any artificial means to prolong her life. My father's directed me to use any and all measures to prolong his.

I wept due to the shock of getting these emotion-laden documents in the mail from an attorney with no prior discussion. I wept at the thought of my parents' mortality. I wept because if I had my way, I might have reversed their directives.

Distraught, I called my parents. I told my mother I'd never pull the plug on her, and then asked my dad why he chose such extreme measures. He laughed and said, "You know I want to live forever." I filed the papers away, hoping they would never be needed.

That living will signed ten years ago is now taking precedence over the will of the living, as expressed as best my father can when it really matters – as he is preparing to die. I can justify that my father brought this on himself – but that's not fair, as he could not predict his future. He had no idea then what fate might befall him. We never do.

Keep Him Alive

I leave a message for my sister that she should come as soon as possible. She doesn't call me back.

Early this morning I call her again, sobbing, begging her to come now. I tell her of the battle over the living will, that we might be forced to send him to the hospital with tubes and…

"I'll come sometime later today," she says coldly. "Keep him alive until I get there."

I try to tell her that he needs her now, that I need her now. That I can't keep him alive alone. I need someone to share this with, and a sibling is the only one who can fully understand.

Yet I fear her involvement too – fear her flying in like a bat out of hell, wanting to be seen as the one in charge and reversing decisions I have made. Yet, I am also ready to surrender control – I am exhausted, with no reserves left.

If It Were My Father

Another doctor comes by today and finds my dad to be quite lucid. He talks to him and then asks him again, "Do you want to go to the hospital?" My dad clearly answers, "No." The doctor tells me that from his perspective, my dad is of sound enough mind for his current decision to override the living will.

He tells me that he feels I am doing the right thing keeping this 90-year-old man in a familiar place, especially with his dementia. He tells me he'd do exactly the same if it were his father. He documents his conversation with my father in the chart, so we are back on track for a peaceful, comfortable passage…God willing.

Hobson's Choice

My minister told my sister and me that there's a reason the story of Cain and Abel is among the first in the Bible.

My sister has arrived and is demanding that our father be hospitalized. She cites the living will and is threatening a lawsuit if his directives are not carried out. She says that my father may have declined admittance to the hospital before, but he might not make the same decision now, as he is getting worse. She says if his choices were to stay here and die, or go to the hospital and live, he'd decidedly choose the hospital. I argue that those are unfair and inaccurate pairings from which he would be asked to choose. He may very well die in the hospital.

Torn between two warring sisters and the threat of a lawsuit, the nursing home administrator decides that the psychologist should interview my dad to definitively determine if he is competent enough to make the decision himself.

I sit off to the side as the psychologist asks him his name, his occupation, his residence – but the morphine precludes answers. The psychologist then crudely asks him, "Do you want to die?" My father, frightened by the question, answers, "No." "Do you want to live?" is answered affirmatively. His response to "Do you want to go to the hospital?" is not decipherable. The choices and the morphine have confused him.

I silently weep as I observe this charade, and I express my discontent to the psychologist. Yet I am forced to face the fact that my father's living will will override any decision we might make in his best interest today.

No Second Chances

"Sometimes we don't get second chances, do we, Dad?" I ask as I cling tightly to his hand.

I weep to think I won't have another chance to take him to breakfast. My sister won't have another chance to spend time with him. He won't have a second chance to change his life in any way. To change his living will.

Sometimes we just hit the end and don't see it coming. That's it – no more opportunity to get it right, to make it better. A course is set, and there is no turning back.

Sometimes we don't get second chances. *Do we, Dad?*

Torture

Too much science; too little comfort.

My father is taken by ambulance to the hospital, and the torture (masquerading as treatment) begins. Although I tell my sister I will not be a party to this, and even say farewell to my father, I remain to witness him howling in pain as they insert tubes and needles into his half-dead body.

With the bright lights shining on his face and the strange surroundings, he is scared and becomes aggressive. But the nurses are only doing what they are obligated to do – save a life no matter the cost. Eight hours later, he is admitted.

I watch his terror and agitation as the tests continue.

Two days later, a doctor tells us that it would be cruel to administer any more treatment.

You'll Know

When you send reiki, you envision the recipient and
ask, "Is this a good time for you to receive reiki?"
During my induction, I asked the masters, "How will I
know if it is not a good time?" They responded, "You'll
know."

Tonight I attempt to send reiki to my dad. With my right hand in the air, I ask, "Is this a good time for you, Daddy?" feeling foolish, knowing that he is lying in a hospital bed. Suddenly, my hand feels excruciating pain. I can no longer hold it in position. As I drop it, I decide to continue with the verbal messages when all of a sudden I start gagging and coughing. I am unable to continue the send.

I assume I am getting a cold, so I go to sleep. The next morning, I am fine – no cough or cold, no pain.

I don't know why it wasn't a good time for him to receive reiki, but the rejection of the healing energy is unmistakable. I suspect he has decided to take matters into his own hands.

Goodnight, Daddy

How many nights in the past 16 months have I said goodnight to my father, promising to return the next day? I'd leave him in the care of his aides and tell him, "I love you. I'll be back tomorrow." He'd always be angry or sad. Now he is silent.

No more visits or rides or dinners. But I have so many memories of our time together. The day before he got sick, I took him for a long ride. We sang along with Dean Martin to *Volare*, and he read all the road signs along the way. We returned to the nursing home and had dinner together, with him merely picking. We watched

Animal Planet and when he got tired, I took him to his room.

The rest is foggy for some reason. I cannot remember our last goodbye as he lay in his little nursing home bed. Was it like all the others or was there something significant about it? I don't know. I only know that his descent began the next morning.

When I visited him at the hospital last night – after he was knocked out by morphine all day – he opened his eyes and mouthed, "I love you" one more time.

And today, I say it to him one final time, as I cover him up: "Goodnight, Daddy. Sleep well. I love you."

My sister and I then leave his body in the hospital, awaiting the gurney.

Just One Little Candle

When I arrive home from the hospital, I find that Peter has lit a candle for my father, a most sensitive gesture that feels so right at a time that is so wrong. Frank leaves a message of sympathy, closing with, "I'll light a candle for him."

I don't know why that grips me so, why it moves me to tears. But it does. It is so simple yet so powerful. The imagery is so strong that I light a candle myself for my dad. It seems mystical and warm – transcending the time and space between us now. The candle feels like a way to communicate with the spirit world.

I am reminded once again how important even the simplest of gestures is at a time like this.

Today

Where to go?
What to do?
It's all nothingness.

There is no point to anything.

What is important now?
I stare vacantly around me.
My thoughts imprisoned in my brain.
I can't sort them out coherently.

Even grieving does not make sense.
What would be the point in that?
For whom or what am I grieving?
Myself?

Today is meaningless.
Nothing I could do would matter.
All I know is that my father is dead.
As of today.

Death Clothes

I gather them all up – the clothes I wore at various stages of my father's dying process. The clothes I wore as I sat at his bedside, lay in bed with him, stood anxiously over him, stroked his head, and held his hand. The sweatshirt with words he read out loud. The socks, the jeans.

I gather up all the death clothes and wash them. Wash the smell and pallor of death away. Wash away the memories, the heartbreak. Wash away the particles of death that desperately cling to the fabric.

Death was in the air and surrounded me. It was in my clothes, on my hair. It was tangible, palpable. Death permeated every fiber, every pore. It came to get my father – became part of my father. And in that way, it became part of me too. Until I wash it away – for now.

Phone Neutralized

Tonight, there is no reason to have my cell phone on. There are no imaginable crises left – no fear of a parent being sick or dying.

All my worries and attentiveness in the world couldn't prevent what happened.

So I turn off the phone – and start breathing again.

No More Tears

I awake in a panic.
I have to get up.
I have to go to work.
No – I have to go to the nursing home.
No – I have to go to the hospital.
No – I have nowhere to go.

My father is dead.
Still today, he is dead.
My stomach is inside out.
My brain barely registers any thought.
My dad is gone.
And I can't even cry.

I carry the tissue box around with me, expecting a torrential
    downpour.
But there are no more tears.
Sadly though, there are regrets.

Regrets for not realizing sooner that he could not eat.
He'd try, just to please me.
And then he'd choke.

I'd comfort him.
But then push food again.
I thought him willful.
He was not.
Damn it!
Why didn't I learn that lesson the first time around?

I did learn it – but my desire to save him was so much stronger
    than cognitive reality.
So here I sit.
Orphaned by the second death.
Dry eyed and flat.
I have no more tears.
Only a broken heart.

Parallel Lives

I struggle to think of someone to call to tell them my father died. His birth family is all gone, and I don't know how to contact the few distant relatives that remain. My sister has called my mother's relatives. So I leaf through my mother's address book and call their friends.

The first, in Florida, has gone to Boston for some medical treatments. The second, my father's college roommate who was so supportive when my mother died, is not available; he himself had a stroke and is in a nursing home. His wife tells me how terrible it is – feeding tubes and all – and how they cry all the time when together. The third tells me she had just lost her husband a few weeks ago. A fourth tells me her husband is having surgery later that week.

Similar fates befall us all in parallel lives. The news of my father's passing is just another drop of sadness into others' own overflowing pools of loss and grief.

While they are sad, their capacity for grief is all filled up. They are now at the age when they are anticipating their own demise. Nick's passing just makes it all the more real.

We are all dying – it's just a matter of when and how the final breath is drawn.

The funeral parlor was filled with his former students,
who regaled us with stories of how much they loved him
as a coach and teacher.

Breathing

I am barely breathing.
My chest barely moves up and down.
So slight the air through my nostrils.

Sometimes I feel like I could just stop breathing.
And have – for short periods.
Like it doesn't matter if I breathe or not.

Air doesn't even seem to get down to my lungs.
It just flows in little streams in and out of my nostrils.
Not really contributing to my life force.

It takes too much energy to breathe.

A deep breath seems to wipe me out.
It hardly seems necessary.

Too much time and attention has gone elsewhere.
There has been no opportunity for me to breathe.
It is long past time to put on my own oxygen mask.

Today, I Bury My Father

> *We buried him in that red sweater my mother liked him
> in so much. And a cap. He looked so dapper, as always.*

Today, I bury my father.
In a hole, next to my mother.
Leave him there.
In the ground.

I tell him I'll be back tomorrow.
As I always did.
I will be back tomorrow, but he isn't really here.
He's dead and buried and gone.

Why am I dry eyed?
So much grief and desperation.
In such a short time.
I must be all cried out.

What would he want?
A grieving daughter who is rendered useless?
Or a fun, lively daughter who can give testimony to his
        spunk?
Some of each, I suspect.

Wheels of Life

baby carriage
stroller
scooter
wagon
tricycle
bicycle
roller skates
skateboard
car
mini-van
motorcycle
tricycle
ambulance
wheelchair
gurney
hearse

Part Fourteen: The Second Time

The Second Time

The second time is different.
Yet, sadly it is familiar territory.
You know what to expect when that last breath is drawn.
You have watched a parent die before.
You have held a lifeless body.

But it is no less traumatic.
In fact, you are more desperate.
It is your last parent who is leaving.
You have lost them both.
And you are powerless to hold on.

You are more pathetic too, second time around.
Others look with pity on you.
Some are tired of your story, your bad luck.
They don't want to get too close, for fear it'll rub off.

The grieving is compounded.
The original loss, not yet reconciled, is magnified.

You want to clear up one before you begin the next.
But time does not allow.

It is confusing to grieve both deaths simultaneously.
You grieve different aspects of the relationships.
They were different people.
And you had a different relationship with each.
Yet the impact is similar.

The second time is different.
No better, no worse.
Just different.
And equally devastating.

The Final Goodbye

> *"The bitterest tears shed over graves are for words left unsaid and deeds left undone."*
> *-Lillian Hellman*

I'm leaving now.
I'll be careful driving and won't speed.
And I'll call you when I get home.
Just like always.

Good luck sorting things out between you.
You always joked about your graves being too close together.
You are united again.
For better or for worse.

Ann Marie says you always came first to me.
I hope you know that.

Now it's your turn again.
To take care of me.

We never talked about my life without you.
What it would be like.
How I should cope.
How you'd want me to be.

I only know I feel so pathetic standing over your graves.
So alone, casting such a pathetic pall.
Can you see me standing here sobbing?
A lone figure in a black coat.

So much time to prepare for this.
So little time to prepare for this.
There is no preparation for this.
No rehearsal, just a live performance.

There are deer tracks on the soft earth that covers your
        caskets.
For some reason, that gives me hope and joy.
I live so far away.
That deer will visit when I cannot.

I must go now, although I feel like my job is not yet done.
Shouldn't I tend to your graves?
Shouldn't I do something more?
Is it really over?

The Last to Go

When all are trapped in her castle, the Wicked Witch of the West declares in a menacing tone, "The last to go will see the other three go before her."

A simple yet haunting line, worthy of a witch. She intended to save the cruelest punishment for Dorothy by having her witness the death of her three friends before her own inevitable demise. Such is the paradox of real life: Those who are "lucky" enough to outlive their loved ones suffer the heartache and pain of losing them one by one.

It's a good thing we don't get to choose the order in which we take our leave. I'm not sure I would have chosen to be Dorothy; I had the heart but often lacked the courage. And now I just want to go home.

Surrogate Parent

I am with my dad in the kitchen of my parents' home. My mother has just died, and he is devastated. He wanders aimlessly from room to room, angry, scared, and despondent. My sister and I try to console him, but we cannot spare him that agony.

Then I awaken – awaken to remember that both my parents are dead. And that both were spared the agony of actively participating in each other's deaths. I served as their surrogates in both experiences; I performed the roles of advocate, proxy, worrier, and griever.

My dad already had some dementia by the time his wife died, so he was spared the full impact of life without her. His life had already changed dramatically by living in a nursing home; he saw her infrequently after she got sick, so losing her was lessened by so many other changes in his own life. Hard enough, but not the same.

And as I stood at my father's deathbed, I knew I was standing in for my mother. I was taking the death blows instead of her – I watched death take my father so that she wouldn't have to witness it. She was spared the anguish of helplessly watching her Nicky leave – and he was spared the same.

I never imagined it would have been like this. Both parents had made it their duty to spare their daughters any and all bad things in life. They shielded and protected us as best they could. But they couldn't spare me the greatest horror of my life – being the sentry at each of their passings.

I suffered the loss of each for both. That is perhaps the one sacrifice they have ever asked of me – and it was both my privilege and my burden to comply.

What Memories, Stuff?

> "I'll be really mad at you, Mom, if I have to clean out all
> your crap when you're gone!" I had repeatedly told her
> over the years. "You won't, dolly," she had assured me.
> "I'll have it all sorted out and cleaned up before I die.
> Don't you worry."

I unpack their belongings, which had been waiting in boxes for their return. The china teacups, the glassware, the vases. I fondle each and reminisce about its role in my parents' lives, in my life. The dusty treasures have meaning because of the people with whom they were associated. Stuff holds no inherent memories, except for the people who touched it and you along the way. People give stuff life; people give it value.

So many of these "valuables" are in disrepair. As my mother aged, she had neither the ability nor will to properly care for them. The desk I coveted – nearly came to blows with my sister over – is cracked and scratched. Hardly worth the additional damage it did to our relationship. Stuff can ruin relationships, as well as recall them.

What am I to do with souvenirs of their lives and the sadness they generate in me? Most of the things my parents saved because they were "too good" will soon be on their way to The Salvation Army. And the things I keep will simply become stuff that someone else disposes of for me someday.

Things are just that: things. We all have too many; we all want more. But they are nothing in the end. How sad to part with, but how ludicrous to have, so much stuff. After all, memories are intangible, aren't they?

No Secrets

There are no secrets when you become infirm or die. Your life is laid bare for the entire world (or, perhaps worse, your immediate family) to see. The gems you tucked away in the jewelry box, the letters and cards you treasured, the photos of days gone by, the special things you saved for special occasions – all open to public scrutiny.

Once you are gone, your privacy is gone. Your stuff is pawed through, rejected or snatched up. Dealers decide if your heirlooms have "any worth." Your life becomes chronicled by what you did or did not leave behind.

What is the impact of this knowing on those who are still able to influence what others will someday find? Or do we really think it won't happen to us. Only to those old people…

The Diary

When cleaning out my parents' apartment, I had found my mother's diary in the nightstand. In her unmistakable yet youthful handwriting, she wrote of school, boys, family and friends from 1931-1935. She had kept it at her bedside for almost 70 years, over several relocations.

When I told her at the time that I had found it, she said, "Don't read it." But, as I told her, I cannot honor her directive. It is teaching me who she was before she was my mother. She and I never did "girl talk" – I never asked or heard about her boyfriends and heartbreaks; she barely wanted to hear about mine. But now, I want to know. I am hungry for every little detail about the woman who brought me into this world.

I now know she had a childhood friend named Patty. And that the attraction she felt toward the man who would become my father, the bad boy from the other side of the tracks who upended her bourgeois life, knew no bounds.

Mad at Myself

Mad at myself.
For being tired.
For having no energy.
For not getting anything done.
For being unmotivated.
For not exercising.
For not thinking clearly.
For not feeling well.

Mad at myself.
For being sad.

For grieving.
For not getting over it.
For losing my parents.

Mad at myself.

Regret and Doubt

Oh, my God! Did I just let my father die? Did I give up on him too soon? Were there medical interventions I could have insisted on to save him? If I had been more aggressive as soon as he fell ill, could I have saved him? Could I have bought him more time? Did I selfishly want him to pass so I could get my life back? Was I negligent? In the end, was I a huge disappointment as his caregiver? Did I let him (and my mother) down?

My rational side says no. Doctors have convinced me that nothing could have saved him from the aspirant pneumonia. And he lived 16 months longer than Hospice had initially given him in Florida. Had we brought him through this bout, I'm almost sure he would have relapsed soon thereafter.

But it's that "almost sure" part that trips me up, bringing me to desperate tears. I am left with conflicting guilt over not taking my father to the hospital sooner and over allowing him to go at all. Should I have fought harder to keep him out of the hospital? Should I have called in another expert to get at his true wishes since the psychiatrist's questioning of him was bogus?

I beg my mother to give me a sign of approval or forgiveness for decisions made in my father's final days. I get an answer within minutes of this writing.

One of my mother's dear friends calls from Kentucky to relay to me that she had just given strict orders to the nursing home staff that her father is never to be taken to the hospital. She hopes she made the right decision and checks in with me following my experience.

The call was out of context; the message was not. I wish I had fought harder to let him die in his familiar surroundings, with caregivers he'd known for over a year. I must remember that I did try – it just didn't work out. And if he had not gone to the hospital, I would no doubt be questioning that as well. It's all part of the process.

The Cruelest Season

I'm trying to pretend that Christmas doesn't exist this year – because my parents don't. Last Christmas, I still had two parents. Compromised though they were, I still had them. This year I have none. And where is home? In a Holiday Inn in my hometown?

Christmas carols cut deep, so full of tradition, memories and merriment, promises of love and hope that can no longer be believed once your innocence has been stripped from you.

It strikes me that Christmas is the cruelest season of all. Beginning with the birth of Jesus, the joy of Christmas always devolves into the death of Good Friday. We know what eventually happens to that baby born in a manger, so full of promise. Yet we still celebrate the possibilities his birth portends.

I know that is a metaphor for life, but the shroud of death still looms too large for me to appreciate it right now. Christmas is just one day – another day that doesn't measure up to the promise life holds. Yet I feel immune to further impact on my psyche. I know I can get through Christmas if I've gotten through so much else.

Cards Co-Mingled

Sympathy cards amidst the Christmas cards. Startling to expect one and to find the other, as the neutral envelopes don't give their contents away. I try to sort them into two piles but fail as much as I succeed. The message of joy and God's love butts up against the expressions of sympathy and sorrow understood.

The juxtaposition seems harsh, almost cruel. Christmas letters with generic updates, touting all that is brag-worthy and good about one's life, followed by cards expressing concern for the "challenging year" I have had.

I read each word of each one, appreciative of any personal outreach contained therein. And as I walk away from the two piles, I realize the message in both is really the same: *May light and love surround you and bring you peace and happiness.*

> *I was unable to send acknowledgment cards for over*
> *four months. They made the loss seem too real.*

I Miss Him This Christmas

> *"It's important to remember all aspects of the*
> *complicated relationship with your father," Peter*
> *reminded me.*

I miss him this Christmas.
The man who I always said ruined every Christmas.
The man I dreaded calling on Christmas.
Because he would say mean things about my not being
    there.
I miss him this Christmas.

I miss him this Christmas.

The man who dressed up like Santa Claus for my cousins.

The man who surprised me with the stuffed bear, the pink bicycle, and luggage.

The man who taught me how to ride a bike and drive a standard car.

The man who hummed Silent Night, all year long.

I miss him this Christmas.

I miss him this Christmas.

The playful, grinning man.

The man who loved holiday parades on television.

The man who loved parties.

And was the life of every party attended.

I miss him this Christmas.

Part Fifteen: The Opening Window

The Opening Window

I am concerned that I haven't heard from my father. While my mother has come through loud and clear, my dad has been silent, again playing second fiddle to my mother.

I feel sad but also guilty that I am still more closely aligned with my mother, even in their deaths. I wonder if that will just be the way it is forever between my father and me – a flawed connection, *on earth as it is in heaven.*

Yet upon waking, the song *Daddy's Little Girl* is going round and round in my head. I find myself cheerfully humming it as I get ready for work. I then realize the significance.

That is not a song I ever related to; it was too fraught with the unconditional love I always felt he had withheld. But my dad loved the song, and we danced to it at my wedding.

I don't even remember the lyrics and I never hum, especially not in the morning! But here I am with a song in my head and in my heart, which had to have come from my father – the constant hummer who loved that song so.

Such a gift at exactly the right time. *Thank you, Dad. You're the end of the rainbow.*

Dear Dad

Marie told me that she sensed my father was "hanging around," watching over me and waiting for forgiveness. She suggested that I write him a letter to release him from this earthly plane.

Dear Dad,

Although I thought we were reconciled before your passing, it seems we still have more to say to each other. We had a rocky relationship; that is not to be denied. Mom always said you were a good father; I must confess there were too many times when I did not agree with her assessment. Your temper and volatility scared me. I felt like I could never do enough to please you. I tried so hard not to push your buttons, to stay under the radar. That also resulted in my distancing myself from you, which only enraged you more. In retrospect, I know you were struggling too. Much of your anger was the result of my rejection, and I rejected you because of your anger.

Yet your spirit lives on in me, Dad, in so many ways. I am so grateful for the sense of humor and playfulness you bestowed. Your love of animals gave me a special bond with my dog. You were so handsome, and I like to think that my dark eyes and olive skin are pieces of you. You danced and sang (hummed, really) and were the life of every party. Above all, I know how much you loved me. You were snuggly and affectionate, much more so than Mom, and when I was down, you were there for me.

My fondest memories of you are sadly your last few months of life. Maybe with Mom gone, our hearts could be more open to each other. You became a sweet, gentle old man who lit up when I walked through that door that held you hostage. Sometimes you even clapped when I appeared! Some of our best times together were just sitting and watching TV. Despite your dementia, you always recognized me, and I'm grateful that I never became a stranger to you.

I miss you more than I thought I would, Dad. It surprises me how the grief lingers. In many ways, I miss you more than Mom because you and I had a more active relationship at the end. We went places together and shared experiences. You became a buddy, which is what you had always hoped I'd be to you.

I understand it all so much more now than I did. And I do forgive you, Dad. I hope you forgive me for not being as attentive a daughter as I know you would have wanted. Most importantly, I love you, Dad. Perhaps now more than ever. I love you enough to let you go, something that was hard for you to do for me.

A better place awaits you, Dad. Go. Go! And take my love with you. We'll meet again.

Love,
Patty

Differences

He ate hot dogs; she, yogurt. Battle Hymn of the Republic *was her musical request for her funeral;* Just a Gigolo, *his.*

Would she smile? Would he grimace? As they now observe my behaviors from their new vantage points, how do they react? Are their values the same as they were?

While I sense they now both come from a place of acceptance and non-judgment, their differences are once again accentuated to me as I think of them once more together, watching over me. I feel the distinction – even the tension – stemming from their unique personalities as they silently weigh in on my life.

I find that I am once again trying to please them both at the same time – still a nearly impossible task.

No Tragedies

While meditating tonight, I call upon both my parents to stay close because I still need them. My thoughts drift to my mother dying at 88 and my dad at 90. Although people say those are "ripe old ages," it still seems to me that they were struck down too soon.

Following my mother's lead, I too now call upon my deceased parents for intervention. I ask them to please watch over the passing of a 12-year-old boy who I heard is going to be taken off life support tonight. *Now that's a real tragedy*, I tell them, trying to center myself.

This response comes rapidly forth from my mother:
There are no tragedies, Patty.
There is only life.

Liberated

Funny thing about something bad happening to you. Something you have feared. The fear and anxiety you have felt surrounding the possibility disappear. They lose their grip on you. You no longer have to anticipate and wonder if it will happen... because it already did. You no longer have to position yourself to try to prevent it, to outmaneuver the odds. You no longer have to wonder how it will feel, if you can handle it. There is no need for the dread anymore.

It's over. You are liberated from the torment of not knowing.

But there is more "good" news: The human spirit is resilient, and we do "handle" it. We put one foot ahead of the other and begin the process of dealing and healing. It's not fun, and it drains our reserves. But we do what we have to do and, as painful as it is, we somehow make it through, knowing that we are stronger for the experience.

Lawn Sale

> How my mother loved to have a lawn sale on my
> front yard! She'd bring the crappiest of stuff and set it
> up proudly, holding out for her price. She worked the
> crowd, a true saleswoman, engaging and confident.

Has it really come to this? Selling your belongings on my front lawn? Your precious candlestick holders (cracked, chipped and glued, but precious to you all the same) for $1 and still not purchased. No one even wants the furniture.

It would sadden you as it does me. But I don't know what else to do with the stuff. You were always so generous and gave your daughters so many beautiful things. I treasure them, yet know that someday those too will be sold by the next in line.

I am respectful of the journey these pieces have taken, but possessions have become less and less important to me. And I would trade all material goods for just one more day with you.

Family Style

I can no longer say, "I'm going home for the weekend." Because there is no home there anymore. But there is a network of friends who have become family, and that is why I still go to Rochester.

It's the same drive – the miles click off as I pass the familiar Thruway signs. But the intent of the trip feels so different. I am now an adult going to visit friends, not a child going "home" to see my parents. It starts to get emotionally difficult as I approach the last rest area before the exit. I used to call my parents from that spot to tell them I'd be there soon. My mother would exhort me to be careful, take my time, and watch out for patrol cars.

But today, I pass by that landmark and use my cell phone to call friends who are waiting for me at a restaurant. They too tell me not to rush – they'll wait. They are happy to see me, greeting me with hugs and questions about my life since last we spoke. We have a drink and eat dinner together, gabbing away. If not family, then certainly family style. And although I still feel adrift, with no parental roots and only temporary lodging at the end of the night, I also feel safely grounded in their affection.

Despite my change in status, I still belong in that city, still feel loved and welcomed. A surrogate family has emerged for me as my birth family slipped away. I hadn't realized that such a transition had begun, but cosmic forces were taking care of me through such kind and generous friends.

Spider Lessons

A spider's work is destroyed so easily and quickly. The web is delicate and vulnerable and can disappear without warning within seconds.

Spiders can't afford to grieve their loss; they must rebuild quickly to survive. Equally complex webs appear in what was just hours ago a web-free zone.

Through spiders, nature provides a lesson on resiliency. We can all lose it all. And most of us do at some time or another. The secret of our success lies in how quickly we can rebuild.

And the itsy bitsy spider
Climbed up the spout again.

For Yourself

Dance.
Do reiki.
Exercise.
Be funny.
Dress sexy.
Buy flowers.
Write poetry.
Bake cookies
Light candles.
Go for a walk.
Get a massage.
Wear make-up.
Watch a movie.
Color your hair.
Drink fine wine.
Paint your nails.
Buy nice things.
Play soft music.
Use good dishes.

Cook good food.
Grind fresh coffee.
Read interesting stuff.

For yourself.
Just for yourself.

Live Your Life, Patty

I feel it in the air – there is a mystical connection to be made tonight. I know it is imperative that I meditate, to be open to messages from beyond. Yet I dread it for the tears it will invariably invoke. Still the pull is strong.

I decide to inhale the chakra colors and exhale gray toxins. I finish with violet light on top of my head, the connection with the spiritual universe. Although the room is cold due to furnace problems, I am on fire, including my hands.

I then begin to have flashbacks of my parents' final days and am overcome by the same old sense of despair. Suddenly, interrupting the flashbacks, this message comes through loud and clear:

Live your life, Patty.
Live every minute of it.
It goes by so fast.
Don't wait to do things you want to do.
Let us go, Patty.
Move on.
Live your life.

The source is unmistakably my mother, directing me to move on. And then it is over, this fleeting message from beyond…but it has the power to change my life, as does every word I have written on these pages.

They Live On

In their recipes.
In their tools.
In the stories.
In the traditions.

In our laughter.
In our tears.
In our dreams.
In our memories.
In our choices.

They live on.

Epilogue

Life does not cease to be funny when people die. Life does not cease to be serious when people laugh.
-George Bernard Shaw

At the time, these 18 months seemed like a *Twilight Zone* episode. Yet, as hard as it is for even me to believe, I wouldn't trade the experience. The resulting self-reflection and coming-of-age were transformational. I am changed for the better for having lived it, although there were times I never thought I'd survive it.

If there is a happy ending, it is that I learned so much about life and love. I can now speak of my parents without a catch in my voice; I can heartily laugh out loud again. Yet the imprint of the experience remains on my heart, and I am forever changed. My journaling and searching continue as I work to discover who I am after this experience, deal with broken relationships, and rebuild my life without the people who gave me life.

Dolly, my golden retriever puppy, is training to be a therapy dog for nursing homes. Together we will visit those who give so much more than they get.

If there is a lesson to be drawn from my experience, it is to value every day and never take what you have for granted. To quote my channeled mother: *Live your life. Live every minute of it.*

It goes by so fast. Don't wait to do things you want to do.

And step up to the plate when your time comes to be present. Everyone needs an advocate at the end of life – but more importantly, companionship. We are all stronger in the face of adversity than we realize. We can do almost anything if we care enough about the outcome.

Thanks for letting our story into your life. And remember… they *do* live on. In you. And beyond.

Patty
November 2010

"We'll always remember, dolly," my mother promised.
"We'll always remember."

Meet Mom and Dad

Obituary for Amelia (Dembowski) Nugent

January 2004

All her life, Amelia was an example of how the mind triumphs over matter, but her seemingly indomitable spirit has surrendered at the age of 88.

The daughter of Eugenia and Edward Dembowski, Amelia lived most of her life in East Irondequoit, NY where she ran a prominent real estate brokerage for more than fifty years. She also served on the Real Estate Board of Rochester and worked to rehabilitate homes for low-income families in the city.

Amelia earned a bachelor's degree from Buffalo State College and taught elementary school for several years in New York, Ohio, and Alabama. A tireless advocate for effective and responsible public education, Amelia founded the Taxpayers' Common Sense Committee in the late 1960's, serving on the East Irondequoit Board of Education for six years, two years as president. She wrote and spoke extensively on public education as a syndicated columnist in the *Olean Times Herald* for 20 years, *The New York State Taxpayer* for eight years, and *The Buffalo Courier* for four years. She also appeared on a weekly radio program called *Speaking My Own Mind.*

Never shy of controversy, Amelia was involved in a two-year lobbying effort to convince the NYS legislature to outlaw gender discrimination in employment. The law was changed in 1965. She was listed in *Who's Who in American Women* in 1977 and has an honorary plaque at the National Women's Fall of Fame in Seneca Falls.

Other public service included directorships on the boards of the American Association of University Women, the Rochester Federation of Women's Clubs, The Red Cross, and the Salvation Army, for which she tutored students and rang the bell at Christmas. She chaired the Monroe County UNICEF campaign for seven years as well. She wintered in Largo, Florida with her husband, Nicholas, where she was a frequent contributor to the editorial page, sold real estate, and golfed.

Obituary for Nicholas J. Nugent

November 2004

Nicholas J. Nugent, formerly of East Irondequoit, NY, passed away at the age of 90 after a long and colorful life.

The son of Anna and Steven Nucchi, Nick was an outstanding basketball and soccer player at John Marshall High School and played on Rochester's Lewis Street Center Stars – a team that won 66 straight games. Also on the team was Amos Jacobs, who would later become famous as entertainer Danny Thomas. His team picture hangs in the lobby of St. Jude's Hospital.

Nick earned his degree in physical education from Cortland State Teachers' College, where he was captain of both the soccer and basketball teams, and received his master's degree from Ithaca College. He served as a captain in the US Army Air Corps during WWII. Nick spent his whole career with the Rochester School for the Deaf as coach and head of physical education, producing many championship teams. He retired as athletic director in 1973 and joined his wife's real estate firm as assistant broker. He was a basketball referee and driver education teacher in the area for over 20 years. Long after he retired, his former students sought him out in both Rochester and Florida. In recent years, Nick wintered with his wife Amelia in Largo, Florida, where he became an avid golfer.

About the Author

Patricia A. Nugent

Patricia A. Nugent was born in Rochester, New York. She attended the State University of New York at Oswego and received a master's degree from the State University of New York at Albany. In addition, she has a recent graduate degree in Communication and Rhetoric from Rensselaer Polytechnic Institute, where she presented papers at national conferences and received literary awards (including one bestowed by Susan Sontag) for her creative nonfiction essays.

She worked as a teacher and school district administrator for over 30 years in upstate New York and has been an adjunct professor at three universities. She continues to train and consult on issues related to human resource management, and interpersonal and organizational communication.

The historic yet humorous play she wrote about the suffragists (*The Stone that Started the Ripple*) sold out all performances and received a stellar review from a respected arts critic. At the Clinton Global Initiative, she facilitated world leaders and celebrities on topics of international concern. However, she believes that her most notable credential is that she was a daughter who ministered to her parents during their final year of life. She considers *They Live On* to be her most important work to date.

Although she has been published numerous times in national professional journals, this is her first creative nonfiction project to be made available to the general public.

Ms. Nugent, a reiki master, lives in Saratoga Springs, New York with her golden retriever, Dolly, who is training to be a therapy dog for nursing homes.

For information about group book sales or to schedule a reading for your organization, contact Ms. Nugent at info@theyliveon.org.